"With this collection, Shanee Stepakoff finally breaks the veil of silence that surrounds the unspeakable horrors of Sierra Leone's long civil war. She has recomposed the official accounts to offer us both the intimacy and eternality of survivor stories."

—Remi Raji, author of *A Harvest of Laughters*

"Of the many forms of human suffering, ethical loneliness—the experience of enduring atrocity only to be confronted with the annihilating cruelty and injustice of remaining unheard—sheds a radiant, hurt light on the very nature and power of language itself. In stark, beautifully calibrated lines, Shanee Stepakoff reaches into that silence to serve and bring forth these necessary voices. Here, the plainest words—'I saw,' 'I heard,' 'I walked,'—take on an almost shocking and devastating dignity. As the survivors recount their stories, it is as if each syllable, each word, is a bone stripped bare. At once unsparing and informed by a deep tenderness and care, this darkly luminous work implicitly interrogates the nature of authorship and poetic form, and like all seminal works, helps to question, expand, and redefine their boundaries."

—Laurie Sheck, author of *Island of the Mad*
and *A Monster's Notes*

"When politics invades lives in the most brutal of ways, what can be fashioned from the aftermath? In these found poems Shanee Stepakoff has taken the testimonies of those upon whom the violence was committed and turned them into a work of witness, Nadine Gordimer's 'inward testimony' that it is the task of artists to deliver. Outwardly the poems in this collection stand as monument to remembrance and commemoration, a stay against oblivion for the people of

Sierra Leone whose lives were marked by the civil conflict of 1991–2002. They are a significant contribution to the literature of that country and of conflict."

—Aminatta Forna, author of *Happiness*

"The incredible horrors painfully recited herein, including the mutilation of children, mass rapes, and torture by rival revolutionary groups makes us wonder whether humans are really human. Shanee Stepakoff's documented testimonies illustrate the continuing crying need for effective international controls and binding laws to deter such atrocities everywhere."

—Benjamin Ferencz, investigator of Nazi war crimes after World War II and the last surviving Nuremberg prosecutor

"These 'found poems' are unquestionably harrowing to read and painful to absorb. Eight survivors of the murderous cruelty and atrocities committed during the civil war in Sierra Leone tell their own stories, and in their own words. Every one of these words is drawn from transcripts of the war crimes tribunals that came with the end of that war. Shanee Stepakoff—a psychologist who has long worked with survivors of torture—brings to these transcript accounts her poet's sense of lineation, stanzaic structure, pauses, refrains, and repetitions. Thus, she creates a ceremonial space in which we as readers might begin to hear and bear witness to the unbearable degree of violence, suffering, and loss that these women and men endured."

—Fred Marchant, author of *Said Not Said: Poems*

Testimony

Oct. 9, 2021

For Ben Ferencz,
with gratitude and with
every best wish—

Shanee Stepakoff

The Griot Project
Founding Editor: Carmen Gillespie, Bucknell University
Series Editor: Cymone Fourshey

This book series, associated with the Griot Project at Bucknell University, publishes monographs, collections of essays, poetry, and prose exploring the aesthetics, art, history, and culture of African America and the African diaspora.

The Griot is a central figure in many West African cultures. Historically, the Griot had many functions, including as a community historian, cultural critic, indigenous artist, and collective spokesperson. Borrowing from this rich tradition, the *Griot Project Book Series* defines the Griot as a metaphor for the academic and creative interdisciplinary exploration of the arts, literatures, and cultures of African America, Africa, and the African diaspora.

Expansive and inclusive in its appeal and significance, works in the *Griot Project Book Series* will appeal to academics, artists, and lay readers and thinkers alike.

Selected Titles from the Series

Testimony

~

Found Poems from the Special Court for Sierra Leone

SHANEE STEPAKOFF

FOREWORD BY ERNEST D. COLE

Lewisburg, Pennsylvania

Library of Congress Cataloging-in-Publication Data

Names: Stepakoff, Shanee, author.
Title: Testimony : found poems from the special court
for Sierra Leone / Shanee Stepakoff.
Description: Lewisburg, Pennsylvania : Bucknell University Press,
2021. | Series: The Griot Project book series.
Identifiers: LCCN 2020044884 | ISBN 9781684483105 (paperback) |
ISBN 9781684483112 (cloth) | ISBN 9781684483129 (epub) |
ISBN 9781684483136 (mobi) | ISBN 9781684483143 (pdf)
Subjects: LCSH: War crime trials—Sierra Leone—Poetry. |
Sierra Leone—History—Civil War, 1991–2002—Poetry. |
Sierra Leone—History—Civil War, 1991–2002—Personal narratives—
Poetry. | LCGFT: War poetry.
Classification: LCC PS3619.T476494 T47 2021 | DDC 811.6—dc23
LC record available at https://lccn.loc.gov/2020044884

A British Cataloging-in-Publication record for this book is available
from the British Library.

♾ The paper used in this publication meets the requirements of the
American National Standard for Information Sciences—Permanence of
Paper for Printed Library Materials, ANSI Z39.48-1992.

www.bucknelluniversitypress.org

Distributed worldwide by Rutgers University Press

Manufactured in the United States of America

Liberia, 1989–2003
Sierra Leone, 1991–2002
for those who died
for those who survived

Since then, at an uncertain hour,
That agony returns:
And till my ghastly tale is told,
This heart within me burns.
　　—Samuel Taylor Coleridge,
"The Rime of the Ancient Mariner"

Contents

Foreword

For more than ten years, from 1991 to 2002, Sierra Leoneans endured the unspeakable ravages of a brutal civil war. Characterized by amputations, arson, and gruesome atrocities such as the disembowelment of pregnant women and decapitation of innocent civilians, the war is reputed to have been the dirtiest in the history of West Africa. Needless to say, at the end of hostilities the world was confronted with a deeply traumatized nation, one that was reeling not only from extensive human rights abuses but also from the daunting prospect of picking up the pieces and reconstituting a broken and divided society on the brink of collapse.

As the war ended, the world feared that Sierra Leone could slide back into mayhem if the conditions that precipitated the conflict were not fully and properly addressed. Thus, among the key tasks facing the nation were reconciliation and subsequent reconstruction. There were several questions in the minds of Sierra Leoneans: How can we as a nation come to terms with this wanton demonstration of violence and on such a scale? In the aftermath, are forgiveness and compassion even warranted? How can we hold those responsible for massive human rights violations to account without tipping the scales of justice to legitimize retribution and vengeance? Would it ever be possible for survivors and perpetrators to coexist meaningfully and productively in postconflict Sierra Leone and, if so, on what basis and under what conditions?

Given the nature of the abuses and the length of time over which they were committed, the country needed a system or structure to identify the civil war's causes and to assist perpetrators and survivors in making a transition to a post-conflict society. One way to do this was to establish a Special Court that would be charged with holding to account those who bore the greatest responsibility for crimes committed during the mayhem. This system of accountability also made provisions for storytelling as a basis for individual and societal transformation, albeit to a somewhat lesser extent than the Sierra Leonean Truth and Reconciliation Commission (TRC).

As a Sierra Leonean, I can attest to the significance of storytelling in our cultural milieu. Stories have a way of opening a space to history, memory, and accountability. They provide a canvas for society to revisit and examine the place where history and memory intersect with human action and choices, as well as the consequences of those choices. Above all, they are a mechanism for reinvention and transcendence. As survivors tell their stories, they inhabit a space that offers opportunities to grapple with and overcome the past and explore their present status as witnesses to history. In this capacity, individuals prove they have survived and are now in a position to reconfigure new identities and offer a basis for collective engagement and for seeking a balance between accountability and reconciliation. The Special Court in Freetown offered both perpetrators and survivors the opportunity to revisit the past in the hope of bringing new understandings of the present.

In the mandate of the Special Court, storytelling offered survivors and perpetrators a mechanism for at least some measure of psychological mastery and restitution, however imperfect. Through storytelling, the fragmented pieces of survivors' lives might begin to be reconstituted, the scars and wounds of society could be partially healed, and the spiritual and physical brokenness rendered whole again, given adequate time and space for mourning. Culturally, Sierra Leone has deep indigenous wellsprings of spirituality, resilience, sense of community, and mutual support among neighbors and extended family as resources for coming to terms with the past and facing the present and future.

After such a long and agonizing war, total recovery might not be possible for individuals nor for society as a whole. Nevertheless, publicly sharing about the human rights abuses may be a useful step toward preventing such abuses in the future and obtaining reparations and redress should violations recur. The witnesses whose voices are represented in this collection made the choice to recount their experiences in a public forum where they were heard on the radio and quoted in local newspapers. In this book, Shanee Stepakoff aims to bring an awareness of the Sierra Leone Civil War and its painful impact to a wider audience. These poems make it possible to accomplish this critical objective.

Through the medium of poetry—specifically, poems derived from actual testimonies—events from the war are conveyed with potency and memorability. Though she is not a Sierra Leonean, Shanee Stepakoff through her use of "found" language has managed to discern and disclose some important truths about the war, including a number of atrocities that have not yet been described by poets from within the region. This book uses the testimonies of trauma survivors to create pace and meaning through visual and sensory devices. The collection is at its best in generating a context for interpretation using the survivors' language of pain, resilience, and transcendence. In isolating critical moments of the atrocities, the author brings a quality of acuteness and intensity to the witness reports. In consequence, readers gain greater insight into the impact the war has had on individuals, families, and communities. Further, readers learn about specific meanings that bodily scarring and disfigurement may carry for individuals and the wider society. Through poetic elements such as line breaks, space, and imagery, the author opens up a new method for the literary representation of trauma and pain.

In this collection, Shanee Stepakoff uses language successfully to unearth the buried voices of victims and survivors. In so doing, she elevates human dignity and fosters in readers a deeper empathy for war-affected women, men, and children in Sierra Leone as well as in the Sierra Leonean diaspora. Through repetition, appropriate diction, and words placed in specific and strategic points in the poems, along with tenor, tone, pace, and parallel structures that heighten mood and atmosphere, the author captures the rhythm and nuances of the English language as spoken by Sierra Leoneans. The influence of the vernacular Krio on the poetry's semantic and syntactic structures, and the deliberate line breaks that accelerate or decelerate the narrative, are effective. It is my hope that this collection will contribute to the emerging corpus of literature of trauma in postconflict societies in Africa and shed light on the complexities of peace building and reconciliation after the horrors of civil wars.

Ernest D. Cole
August 2020
John Dirk Werkman Professor of English
Hope College, Holland, Michigan

Notes on the Text

Within the poems, a three-dot ellipsis indicates a pause in the testimony. Such pauses signify that at that moment, the witness had begun to cry. At such moments, the judges usually granted a short break so that the witness might regain his or her composure.

The word "Kamajor" (featured in several poems) is pronounced with a soft "a" in the first and second syllables, a hard "o," and a silent "r," with the accent on the first syllable, namely, as "káhma-jo." In Sierra Leone, the first two letters of "junta" (a word used several times in one poem) are pronounced in a manner similar to the "j" and "u" in "justice."

The eighth poem in this collection is based primarily on the witness's testimony for the RUF prosecution on the dates indicated. This witness (TF1-097) also gave evidence in the Charles Taylor Trial, which the SCSL conducted from 2007 to 2012. The poem incorporates some components from his testimony of October 16 and 17, 2008 in that trial.

English was the court's working language, and all official transcripts are in English. Most witnesses, however, testified in one of ten local languages (Mende, Temne, Krio, Limba, Mandingo, Kono, Fula, Kissi, Kuranko, Susu). Sierra Leonean courtroom interpreters provided simultaneous translation between these languages and English. Hence, the poems composed from the transcripts encompass not only the words of the witnesses but also those of the interpreters. Rarely, there were slight errors in the language interpretation. In these instances, I chose the more accurate term over the term in the official record. Also, infrequently, if an exact synonym could be used that had better rhythm and sound for the stanza, I opted for the synonym. I felt that this was justified given that the various interpreters each had their own preferences for particular words and phrases. In addition, in some instances I substituted a standard English word for a Krio term to enhance intelligibility for readers unfamiliar with Krio.

Testimony

Introduction

Silence, Language, and the Making of Art

Historical Context

The poems in this collection were composed directly from the official, public transcripts of the Special Court for Sierra Leone (SCSL). The SCSL was a war crimes tribunal established jointly by the United Nations and the postwar Sierra Leonean government, with the mandate of bringing to trial those believed to bear the greatest responsibility for war crimes and crimes against humanity committed during the Sierra Leone Civil War.

The war began in 1991, when the Revolutionary United Front (RUF)—with the backing of Charles Taylor, a prominent warlord who later became president of Liberia—crossed Sierra Leone's eastern border and launched a series of attacks to overthrow President Joseph Momoh. By seizing control of the coveted diamond fields, the rebels were able to buy weapons to widen the war. During the following decade, there were three military coups, a failed peace agreement, and a rebel invasion of the capital, Freetown, in which over 5,000 people were killed.

The war was characterized by massive human rights abuses. The deliberate terrorization of entire villages and towns by the various warring factions was routine. More than 50,000 civilians were killed, and untold numbers were maimed. Over 500,000 fled to neighboring countries, and a quarter million more were internally displaced. In 2001 the rebels and the government signed a new peace agreement, and by January 2002 the war was finally over. Presidential elections were held in May 2002 and were widely reported to have been free, fair, and peaceful. The Special Court was launched later that year.

Over 300 witnesses gave evidence in the SCSL trials. At the conclusion of the first three trials (between 2007 and 2009), convictions were entered against the senior commanders of the three main factions that had participated in the war (the RUF, Armed Forces Revolutionary Council, and Civil Defense Forces). For security reasons, the fourth, and final, trial—that of the former Liberian president, Charles Taylor—was conducted in The Hague. He was convicted in April 2012. All those who were convicted received long prison sentences. In December 2013 the Special Court, having completed its mandate, closed.

My decision to use "found poetry" in a postwar setting was grounded in a series of formative experiences that began in young adulthood. Below, as I trace the unpredicted trajectory of those experiences, I touch upon complex interactions among violence, vicarious trauma, silence, language, and the making of art.

First Exposure, Secondhand Trauma

From 2005 to 2007, I was the SCSL's psychologist. But my connection to political violence on the African continent had begun twenty years earlier. I was first exposed to human rights abuses in 1986 in South Africa, during the height of apartheid-era repression, when anti-apartheid activists were being systematically targeted and killed. I was twenty-three years old, completing an internship for a master's degree in psychology. Most of my closest colleagues were survivors of torture and related forms of state-sponsored violence. Drawing on interviews with them and with others to whom they referred me, I conducted a detailed, qualitative study of the experiences and coping strategies of South African political detainees.

In 1988 and 1989, I photocopied my thesis, replacing my name with a pseudonym to protect the identities of those I had interviewed, and distributed these copies to mental health professionals in South Africa, Latin America, and Asia, as well as the library of the International Rehabilitation Center for Victims of Torture in Copenhagen; and I presented portions at the national convention of the American Psychological Association. Numerous colleagues and readers urged me to publish a book, an article, or both.

Yet these harrowing accounts of the torture of men, women, and children by the South African government remained in a file cabinet for over two decades, untouched and unseen. Even after apartheid had ended and the South African Truth and Reconciliation Commission was established, I did not open my file drawer, though I knew the detailed testimonials I had collected could serve as important documentation of apartheid-era crimes, buttressing the testimony given by survivors during the TRC proceedings.

It took more than a quarter century for me to articulate this, but in retrospect, I recognize that I too experienced a form of trauma from listening to survivors' accounts. With my colleagues in South Africa, I had been able to verbally process my impressions and responses, but upon returning to the United States to pursue psychology doctoral studies,

I found no one in my environment who could understand or relate to the stories I was "holding"—holding, literally, in my file cabinet, as well as psychologically, in my mind.

At that time in my life, I had not yet claimed an identity as a writer—a person deeply committed to rendering experience in words. So my response was to refrain from speaking at all, to bury the stories—along with their proof of the survivors' fortitude and resilience. It would take another series of rather improbable events for me to open the file cabinet and begin to reengage with these realities.

Missing Words

After my internship in South Africa and a year of work with Liberian war-trauma survivors in the refugee camps of Guinea, I was hired as the psychologist for the UN-backed war crimes tribunal in Sierra Leone. I remained at the Special Court for twenty-eight months, responsible for providing psychosocial support to witnesses. I often met with them before their testimony, accompanied them in the courtroom as they gave evidence, and debriefed them afterward. And, as part of a study on the long-term psychological impact of testifying in the tribunal, I interviewed them several months later.

Meanwhile, my inchoate interest in writing began to crystallize and intensify. Through a combination of effort and luck, I crossed paths with some poets and writers. When they became aware of my work at the Court and my interest in writing, they would invariably ask, "Are you writing about your experiences working with war victims in Sierra Leone?" And well into my second year at the Court, the answer was brief: No.

I simply could not find the language. Paradoxically, the events that were spoken about by witnesses in the courtroom were, from my point of view, unspeakable. According to *Webster's Dictionary*, "unspeakable" is defined as exceeding the power of speech; incapable of being adequately described; defying expression; synonym: unimaginable. The witnesses themselves possessed the courage and capacity to tell their stories, but I was unable to generate my own words to represent the horrors they described. I kept paper and pen at the ready, I set aside time to write, but nothing emerged—no narratives, no poems.

As a member of the Court's witness protection team I was also required to assist in redacting transcripts of witness testimony so that any identifying information was concealed before posting them on the Court's website, where they would become permanently accessible to the public. So, after long days meeting with witnesses and sitting in the courtroom while they testified, I spent many evenings reviewing trial transcripts. One night, alone in my office after everyone else had gone home and the sprawling Court compound was eerily quiet, while reading the transcript of a witness who had been present during the rebels' deliberate amputation of her six-year-old son's arm, I spontaneously began to condense the testimony into poetic form.

I had recently read Gertrude Stein's *Three Lives* and had been impacted by her skillful use of repetition, her ability to empathically enter each protagonist's subjective world, and the concentrated intensity of her language. Using similar literary techniques, I began to distill the witness's account while retaining the core features of her experience. Using only the witness's words in their naturally occurring order, structuring them with traditional poetic devices such as line breaks, stanzas, assonance, and alliteration, I was able to transform a lengthy and cumbersome prose document into a "found poem," composed directly from the official transcript of the trial.

At last I had arrived at a language to utter the unutterable: *the victim's own language*. Through this process of distillation and shaping, a transcript of over seventy-five pages gradually became a poem. In so doing, a voice that might have been unheard or lost amid the tedious legalistic arguments set forth by the opposing attorneys and the panel of judges had been excavated and amplified. Where my vicarious traumatization in the face of these stories had temporarily silenced me, the witnesses' determination to verbally formulate their experiences provided the missing words.

Hearing Voices, Bearing Silences

After that initial effort, Rainer Maria Rilke's series of poems titled "The Voices" became a key source of inspiration. In Rilke's collection, the experiences of the marginalized or wounded were given expression. I modeled my effort on Rilke's, but focused on experiences that were specifically relevant to the Sierra Leone war. I chose to use only prosecution witnesses, though many witnesses for the defense also had compelling stories. And, just as Rilke had called attention to those whose suffering had been obscured, I chose to use only the testimony of victims, with the single exception of a former child combatant, who was both a victim and a perpetrator. Unlike in Rilke's work, however, the final poem here contains only a title and a blank page. This is intended to symbolize the eternal absence of those who were killed, and to visually represent the stark fact that we who remain are forever deprived of knowing what they might have wished to tell us.

According to the pioneering trauma theorist Judith Herman, silence—the absence of language—is a core component of trauma. What is required for the repair of individual psyches in the aftermath of severe atrocities, as well as for the repair of the communities and countries in which individuals are embedded, is both a language and an audience. Indeed, autobiography theorist Leigh Gilmore describes the presence of a narrative and a listener as the constitutive elements of the testimonial form. The survivor must not merely speak but rather must address other people—specifically, those who are not only willing but *determined* to hear and to know. This is the broader, deeper meaning of testimony. To bear witness does not necessarily imply participating in a legal or juridical proceeding. To bear witness implies the existence of a speaker, a committed listener, and a language.

Yet even when speakers do narrate their experiences to attentive listeners, over time many details fade from public awareness as survivors attempt to rebuild their lives and as the wider community (both local and global) starts to focus on other priorities. As I became aware of the risk that these voices would become less vivid in the minds of listeners/readers and in the historical record, I realized that Stein's technique of repetition could make it possible for readers to stay mentally and morally present to the anguished (and anguishing) reports. Additionally, intentional written repetition seemed compatible with the penchant many Sierra Leoneans show for restating the main components of an oral narrative. Further, the reiteration of specific phrases hints at a quality displayed by trauma survivors in a wide range of settings when they mentally reflect on or speak aloud about their experiences: namely, to revisit those aspects that are hardest to fathom.

During the period I created these poems, I had no conscious knowledge of Charles Reznikoff's work composing found poems from the transcripts of the war crimes tribunal at Nuremberg and the Eichmann trial in Jerusalem. When, much later, I stumbled upon his book *Holocaust*, I was struck by the similarities between his project and mine. I became even more intrigued when I discovered an uncanny coincidence: Reznikoff had published an earlier collection, based on criminal proceedings in the United States, with the same title I had already chosen for the Sierra Leone poems: *Testimony.*

I had to ask myself, *How is it possible that two individuals writing about events that took place in such different eras and in very different parts of the world arrived at the same method of making poems that attest to these events?* As I read more about Reznikoff's process of composing the Holocaust poems, and as I continued to reflect on my own experiences in South Africa and Sierra Leone, I gradually gained a deeper understanding of the impulse to use found language in poems about war and mass violence: we were attempting to structure and contain the horror of the accounts by giving them aesthetic form.

Eventually, I concluded that there may be something specific to situations of large-scale violence that leads poets to draw from preexisting language rather than generate entirely new utterances. In situations of atrocity, one function of the writer is to bear witness. Yet many writers find it impossible to describe the events they have encountered. Perhaps this is why Charles Reznikoff waited until thirty years after the Holocaust to compose his found poems about victims.

Found Poetry: Origins and Innovations

Eventually, I came to learn that while Reznikoff was an early trailblazer of this literary genre, his approach was derived from a larger tradition that became a recognized art form during the early twentieth century. "Found poetry" is defined as the selection and rearrangement of words, phrases, or passages contained in extant sources and reimagined as poems. A found poem begins to emerge as a reader or listener attunes to poetic properties within a text. Variations on this approach have been used in the aftermath of mass violence across cultures and eras. There are moving examples based on texts from the Atlantic slave trade, the Armenian genocide, anti-Jewish pogroms in the Russian Empire, the American Civil War, and more recently, the Iraq War as well as racial violence in the United States. This approach to poem-making shares with found art in other modalities the aims of contributing to public awareness of the realities of war and generating creative responses. Though the antecedents of found poetry are more than a century old, there has been growing interest during the past two decades as the Internet, social media, and smartphones have made it possible for more and more people to gain access to public documents.

Found poetry in general, and even more so in contexts of war, raises important questions about how we define art, artists, and the artistic process. For example, is the poem already present in the preexisting words, which usually were written or spoken by individuals who would not think of themselves, or be thought of by others, as "poets"? Or does a work of literature emerge only when a person trained in the writer's craft arranges the material in a particular way and presents it in a new context? Moreover, this genre requires replacing the commonly held perception that a poem is made by a solitary individual. For instance, a thorough consideration of Reznikoff's *Holocaust* poems must include recognition that the language he borrowed from transcripts was derived partly from the word choices of the language interpreters who translated the witnesses' original words into English. This method of making poems also raises questions about who has the right to broaden the audience for a particular voice—only the person who originally spoke the words, or others who listened closely, found literary value in them, and arranged them in stanzas? Some might posit that a poet should not draw on phrases that he or she did not generate at the outset, whereas others would make precisely the opposite argument: that those who are privileged enough to have access to avenues for publication and dissemination have not only a right but a responsibility to revive the voices that are at risk of disappearing, particularly when the original speakers had only a limited audience, if any at all.

The genre of found poetry fosters a heightened respect for the many ways of using words and the distinctiveness of every voice. Writers who appreciate the poetic potential in descriptions of wartime experiences, however, must not lose sight of the profound losses that inform these descriptions. Readers/listeners, too, have a moral responsibility to apply a special quality of empathic attentiveness to works derived from collective trauma. By summoning this quality, each one of us can become more aware of the horror and the heroism that are present in equal measure in contexts of war.

Reclaimed from the Realm of Shadows

Paradoxically, experiences of severe trauma simultaneously foster a profound *need* for words and a profound *absence* of words. This is why the making of found poetry is both powerful and necessary. Where new phrases cannot be generated, preexisting ones can be recognized, recontextualized, and resurrected.

In giving poetic form to a previously unstructured account, an author provides a container for the speaker's experiences and emotions, which might otherwise seem uncontainable. In many instances, undistilled prose allows readers to ward off the full effect of what has been said. By contrast, when a writer has shaped the material into a literary work, most readers maintain a greater level of recognition and responsiveness regarding the speaker's experience. In this manner, the poet becomes a medium: an instrument through which survivors speak for themselves, but in a clearer and more concentrated manner than would occur in ordinary discourse or protracted court proceedings.

The Russian poet Osip Mandelstam wrote, "I have forgotten the word that I wanted to say, and my thought, unembodied, returned to the realm of shadows." I am suggesting here that we reverse this quote: *I have found the word that I wanted to say, and my thought—now embodied—is reclaimed from the realm of shadows.* Just as the direct victim has a need to tell his or her story to receptive listeners in a public forum, so too does the listener have a need to tell about what he or she has heard.

Using found language and artful choices, I aimed to make poems that would attest to the experiences of the witness, to the wider realities of the Sierra Leone war and the suffering (as well as the dignity, courage, and strength of spirit) of the millions of people who were affected by it, and, more broadly, to the horrors of war. Perhaps, too, bringing forth these poems makes it possible, in some small measure, for me to share with others my experience of bearing witness to the experiences of the witnesses during the years that I worked closely with them and listened to their stories.

Ten years after the liberation of the death camps, Theodor Adorno remarked that after we encounter the enormity of Auschwitz, it becomes impossible to write poems. This collection constitutes a response to that argument: in situations where we are unable to generate language that will adequately communicate the realities, it is both our duty and our deliverance to *find* the words among those who were present and have chosen to speak out. And when we find these words, to bring them forth. Thus we exhume the buried truths. Thus we give voice to the unspeakable.

THE AMPUTEE'S MOTHER
(TF1-214, RUF Prosecution, July 13, 14, 15, 2004)

I am a farmer
and my husband is a farmer.
In fact, I can say I was doing the bulk of the job
because my husband was an old man then.
Currently, I have four children.
I have never gone to school.

We went to weed our farm.
I was pregnant at the time.
I woke one morning
and saw people in military uniform,
they had tied a red piece on their heads.

We were sitting down,
we saw people carrying bundles on their heads
coming toward our town.
We asked where they were coming from.
They said the rebels were burning houses
at particular places.

We took our things
and fled into the bush.
After some time
we came back to the town
to look for food.
Pa Issa met me and I saw
both of his arms were chopped off.

I was in the bush for about three months—
myself, my husband, and my children—
till at last I delivered.

The rainy season met us in the bush
and the place was cold.

Whenever it would rain
the place would be very cold.
We were there until the child got sick
because there were no medical people around,
they had all run away.
So I had to lose my child.
My child finally died.

One morning while we were working on the farm
Sundu and others left for the town
to look for mangoes.

Sundu's father was up the hill
and the hill is a kind of advantageous place
because whilst you are there if someone is coming from
    the town
you will see that the person is coming.
We saw Sundu's father coming to our place.
He said he had looked toward the town
and saw smoke coming from the town
and he called me and said "Mama, Mama"
(because he is the nephew of my husband so he used to
    call me "mama")
and he said, "I saw smoke coming from the town."

Then he said, "Look up and see."
We looked up and we saw smoke coming from the town.
We all shouted and said, "Oh my God, they are burning
    our houses
they are burning the town."

Then we left there and we ran farther into the bush
to hide our children.
We hid them and stood elsewhere
where we could see the town.
We had hidden our children.

I was not there but what that girl told us—
the one who went to the town to look for mangoes—
she said, "Rebels met us in town and they caught us."
Then she said, "Well, God saved us."
Sundu—the girl who went to look for mangoes—
showed a mark on her leg where the man said
her leg would be cut off.
She said, "Why I was able to escape
was when the rebels saw the people running away
with bundles on their heads
they went to the people's direction
because they thought the people had some money
or property that they could take
so when they left toward the people's direction
we ran away."

In the evening some elders went back into the town
to look and see what might have happened.
On that day my husband went to the town
and saw one boy had had his arms chopped off.
Yunku Sesay, both his arms had been chopped off.

When our husbands went back to the bush
to tell us that Yunku Sesay's hands had been chopped off
the following day I myself went to the town
because I was told that my sister's child had got missing.
When I reached the town

I met Yunku Sesay lying down
with both arms missing.
Then we were telling him, "Sorry"—
"Sorry, Yunku Sesay,
Sorry"
after which we left the place and went.

I came to the town and saw with my eyes
the houses burnt.
On one occasion in the morning
I stood up and said I'm going to plant my groundnut.
I went to the farm.
After planting my groundnut I returned to the town
to cook for my children.
When I returned to the town
I told my children to go and fetch water
so that we can cook.
I was in the town cooking.

The farm road I used to come to the town,
it is from there the rebels came.
Little did I realize
they had already surrounded the town.
They were so many.

Little did we realize
they had already surrounded the town.

We heard them fire their weapons rampantly
using all sorts of abusive language:
mammy bombo, mammy toto, mammy pima,
referring to the vagina
your mother's vagina.
And they told us to wait.

During that gunfire
a bullet fragment came
and hit my child on the chest—
his chest was oozing blood.
And then a fragment grazed me
on my back.

My child was shouting,
I too was shouting
because of the way
I was getting the heat of it—
it was burning.

After a short while another rebel boy came.
He held me and took my clothes from me,
asked me for money.
He stripped off my clothes and he said,
"You have money."
He held the gun in his arm.
He held me by my clothes.
He stripped the clothes from me
and asked me for money.
I was standing naked.
I told him I don't have money.
He said it's a lie.
Then he pushed me out.
At the same time they entered the house
and took what they wanted to take.

The rebels instructed me to go with them.
They placed us on the veranda.
Myself and my children.
When they placed us on the veranda
my child was crying

because of the fragment that hurt him—cut him.
The other rebel came and saw the child crying.
He saw blood oozing out of his chest.
Then the rebel boy asked: "What is this?"
I told him my child has been hurt by a fragment.
Then he looked at it and said, "This is nothing."

It was not very long before another one came
holding two sneakers in his arm.
He slapped my jaw with them.
He slapped my cheek.
Then he told me to wait.

Yes, my children saw.

We were seated there
when another rebel came running.
So many people were there
on that veranda.
My children were with me.
I was unable to leave them behind.
There was no way for me to escape because the rebels were—
the rebels were present and they were many.
I didn't feel so fine.

That is—that is—in our village
we don't allow that kind of thing.
Even my husband has never done that to me,
to beat me with his shoes.
To take a shoe and beat someone
is only good for a dog—
in our village, we don't do that.

. . .

When we were seated there,
after a while another rebel—
a boy—
came running.
He saw a girl standing by me.
When he saw this girl
he said, "Hey, lie down on the ground."
The girl began to plead.
He said, "Lie down on the ground."
The girl was—started begging.
He told the girl, "Lie down!"

The girl fell to the ground,
he started pulling her clothes off
and removing his pants . . .

Afterwards, he said, "Get up." The girl stood up.
He said, "This girl, we will take her along.
We are taking her away."
They told us to stand up and follow her
under the cotton tree.

. . .

When we arrived at the cotton tree
we saw their boss man there
seated on a rock.
When we arrived at the cotton tree
their commander, their boss man
ordered us to sit on the ground.
I had my child on my back.
Their boss was there
under the cotton tree.
He sat on a rock.

They had tied two men already.
They were properly tied.
They have took their hands
and brought them on their backs
and tied them.
After they were tied
and were lying on the floor
we sat down.

Their boss man—the commander
who sat on the rock—
began to speak:
"Since you say you love a civil government
we are going to chop off your hands,
we will not let you go free.
If we don't chop off your hands,
we're going to kill you."

Well, my heart was in a tremendous situation
because we saw dead individuals under the cotton tree.
One of the men killed there was stripped naked
as he was in his birthday suit.
I tried to look at him
but when I saw him like that
I had to turn my face.
The others were lying down by him.
I cannot tell the number—there were many.
I cannot tell the number.

So the boss man said, "These ones if you don't kill them
cut off their hands
because they say they want a civil government.
If you are ready to cut off their hands
begin with the child

so that they will know
that they will not be spared."

He was referring to my child.

Well, my child—
well, their boss man
had given the order,
said that his hand should be cut.
At that time my child was small,
he didn't understand
what the man was saying.

My child was six years old.

The man told these other rebel boys,
"Go for a machete and come with it."
A rebel boy went.
When he came back he said
he hadn't got a knife.
The boss man ordered him,
"Go fetch a knife,
and when you come with it
start with the little child."

The rebel boy took off
to search for a machete.
When he left, the boss man rose.
When the rebel boy returned
he called the child, "Come."
Then the child begin weeping,
the child begin weeping.
As he was cutting the child,
the child was weeping.

The child was saying
"Oh, mother, they have cut my hand."
"Oh, mother they have cut my hand."

Then the rebel boy threw
my child on the floor.
After he'd cut my son's hand
he came and sat near me.
When he sat near me, he pulled me up,
he said, "Come on, come here."

He laid me on the ground,
he chopped off my hand.
Then he said, "Come on,
get up, go sit down there."
I sat there with my child,
the blood oozing out.

The other man came and said, "Well, now you are
    beautiful.
It is now that you're beautiful.
Right now where you are, you are very beautiful."
And I said, "Eh, no human being can look at me
and say I'm beautiful."

My child was sitting
the blood oozing out
just like a cut has been opened
his body wet
blood all over.
We sat there.

This boy who had chopped off my hand
and had chopped off my child's hand,

when I tried to look at him he said
"If you look at me, I will chop off the other hand,"
so I stopped looking at him.
We were seated there.

Then I was going and I was dropping, you know,
I was kind of dizzy,
dropping as I went along.
As I stumbled and fell
this same man was still chasing me
telling me I'm beautiful now.

When I reached a particular place
I sat down.
My child fainted, and I fell down.
My child was falling down
and he said, "Mama, I want to drink."

He said, "Mama, I want to drink."

At the time there was no water close by.
At that time I was still feeling dizzy.
I sat close to him.
After some time I would get up.
And I told him I was going to fetch water for him
but I was still dizzy.
And I went—I went to one way or another
and I saw a kettle there with some water in it.
I took that water and I came to where
    my child was,
where my child was lying down.
I sat on the floor and I raised him with one hand.
I called him and I sat close to him. ,
I gave him the water.

After *he* drank I drank the rest.
And I sat down on the floor and I told him
to come onto my back so I could strap him.
I strapped him on my back.

As we were going I had this child on my back
and my other child who was behind me
was crying because he was hungry.
I laid him down and I went and fetched one mango.
I came with it, I peeled it
but because there was blood on it
as I wanted to give the child—
as I wanted to give it to him
so he would eat it and become lively a little bit
he would refuse to eat it because, according to him,
there was blood on it.

I told him that you should lie down for the moment
because—because fighting was going on.
As we were lying down there it was not long
when we heard—when we heard someone say, "Time,
     time, time. The time has come, we should go."
We heard some voices from afar
coupled with gun sounds.

I got up, took my child and strapped him on my back.
When I reached a particular place
I laid him down because I was so tired.
When I laid him down there
I found some leaves
and covered his wound with them
to ward off the flies.

I was so tired.

Then I looked for a road
that would reach the farm road
where my husband had gone to work.
But my mate who had escaped
had already gone to the farm
and told my husband,
so my husband came.
He started crying.
My mother also came
and started crying.

My friend Fina Dabo
my mother and my husband—
they strapped the child.
My mother took some water
washed my body of the blood,
the blood that had been on my body.
They strapped me on their back,
and strapped the child on their back
together with me
and took us to the farm.

When we reached the farm
we slept there.
We sought advice
from one old man
because there was no medicine.
The old man said, "in Kono
when they chop off people's hands
we use tobacco leaf
to tie it round the wounded place."

In Kono when they chop off people's hands
we use tobacco leaf.

At that time my husband had tobacco leaves
so he brought them out
and tied them round my wound.

In the morning, I strapped my child on my back
and as the pain was about to overpower me
I would put him down.
After some time I would strap him again on my back.
When he'd start crying I would strap him on my back.
When I'd reach a particular place
I'd put him down.
That's how we went
until we reached one village—
that's where we slept.

In the morning we went.
As we entered the town
the townspeople said,
"It is good that you have tried hard to reach here.
There's a helicopter on its way.
When it comes it will take you along.
It is good that you tried hard to reach here."

It was not long before we heard the chopper,
the sound of the chopper
and the chopper landed in the field.
They took us where the chopper was
and we came here to Freetown.

When we came here to Freetown
we were taken by car
to a hospital.
The day that we reached here
that was not the day they did the operation.

On the Monday, they took me to the theater
and I was operated on.
Myself and my child.

After long, one day the child asked me—
asked me, "Mama, when will my hand grow again?"

After long, one day the child asked me—
asked me, "Mama, when will my hand grow again?"

After long, one day the child asked me—
asked me, "Mama, when will my hand grow again?"

THE CHILD SOLDIER
(TF2-021, CDF Prosecution, November 2, 3, 4, 2004)

I was born in Kailahun,
Pendembu village.
There I was born. There I stayed with my
    mother.

I was nine years of age
when the rebels attacked the village,
and the rebels captured me.

When the rebels captured me,
I got separated from my parents.
After that, I did not see my parents
anymore.

Before I was separated from my mother
she told me, "My child,
now you are nine years,
you're supposed to be in the fourth grade."
Thus I was able
to know my age.

I was not the only one captured—
they captured most of the boys.

What is a rebel? A rebel is someone
who stays in the bush
who has a gun
but is not a soldier.

The rebels looted the village
where I was captured.

I, along with the other boys they captured,
were given loads to carry to the rebels' base,
which was called Ngeihun. We went to Ngeihun.

We were together with the rebels
in the village of Ngeihun.
When we were caught and brought there,
the rebels used to take
my captured companions and me
around to find food.

The loads that were given to me to carry
were too heavy for me
so I was usually unable
to carry them.
Therefore, on our way for food-finding
we captured civilians
to carry loads for us.

When I was with the rebels at Ngeihun
Kamajors came
and attacked the village.

During that attack,
the Kamajors captured
seven of us little boys
along with three women.

Six of us boys were the same age—
nine or ten years,
and one was fifteen.

Those of us who were captured
were placed on the ground
and told we should sit there.

When the Kamajors captured us,
they entered the huts
and looted some property
and brought it outside,
and then set some houses on fire.

The things that they looted—
some clothes, some seed rice, a tape-player—
they gave us
to carry on our heads.
They said we should come down
to Kenema.

When they gave us the loads to carry
on our heads,
we went through a bush path
and we reached a river called Moi.

There the Kamajors placed the three women
who had been captured
and shot them
and they fell into the river.

They shot the three women.
They fell into the river.

Then we crossed the river.
We used a boat to cross.
There was one boat
with an oarsman

and we took turns
being rowed across the river.
Before we crossed the river,
they killed the three women there.
And then we crossed.

The Kamajors said
they killed the three women
because they were rebels' wives.

Afterwards,
we continued on a bush path
until we entered Kenema.

In Kenema, they took us
to the office of the CDF
at Kaisamba Terrace,
we seven who had been captured.

After a short while
a vehicle came for us.
The man who captured me—
his name was German—
said we were going to his village,
Talia Yawbeko.

We stayed there for some days,
and he told me he was going to initiate me
into the Kamajors.
I told him I'm afraid of being initiated
into the Kamajors.
Then he held my hand,
he took me to the gate
and said, "You see these small boys?

They are all Kamajors
so I don't see any reason
that you should be afraid."
That gave me the zeal.

He held my hand
and took me to the bush.
Before we entered
they placed something in my hand—
a white cloth.

When we entered the clearing
in the woods
we were stripped naked,
all of us.
There were about four hundred
initiates.
Some were around my age
or younger
though most were older than I.
We started to sing.
After the song,
they brought a razor blade
and they started putting marks
on our bodies.

After they had placed these marks
on our bodies,
after they had marked me
all over my body,
there was a black concoction
inside a barrel—
an inky goo.

We would go to that barrel
scoop out the potion
and smear it on our skin.

When we had smeared it on our bodies,
they told us not to bathe for one week.

After the one week had elapsed,
at night, at about two o'clock in the morning
they took us to a graveyard.

In the graveyard
we were told
that if anyone in your family has died,
whether it was your grandfather
or any other family member,
his spirit will come
and give you something—
something not of this world—
which will make you very powerful to fight.
That's why they took us to the graveyard.
We were there until four in the morning.
Then we came back into the bush.

We came back into the bush. We had our bath.
Then it was morning.
On the morning after we had all had our bath,
we came back into the bush.
Forty people were standing on one side
and another forty on the other. All had different canes
in their hands.

We ran between those two lines of people.
As we were running, we were beaten

by the other Kamajors.
They had different canes.
We were running in a line,
and they would whip us.
As they were beating us,
some people collapsed.
As for me, I had some swellings on my body.
My jaw was swollen
and on my body
the skin was coming off.

After they had beaten us,
they made another concoction inside a vat,
which in Mende is called *nesi*—
it's a magic potion.
We each brought an empty bottle
used for locally distilled rum
and they put the potion in it,
but before they did so
they told us that this potion
is our protection
and, when we go to fight,
that's what we should smear on our body
for the fight,
and they gave us a ronko—
a sacred protective shirt.
That's what was given to us
in the ritual space in the woods.

When German took me
to be initiated,
I saw him give palm oil, rice,
and white satin cloth
to the men who were registering our names.

After I had been initiated,
I was taken to Base Zero.
German had to go on a mission.
When he came back,
he came with a gun for me—
a two-pistol grip.

The two-pistol grip
had a handle under and in front,
so you could use that to shoot
without it shaking you up.

When he brought it, he called me.
Then he started teaching me
how to cock the gun and shoot it.

After German gave me that gun,
we went on missions
in the surrounding villages.
We would attack those villages.
We would catch people—women.

The first mission, we went to Masiaka.
The boys, we were many. The older people
were many as well.

When we entered the town,
we started shooting.
The other boy, who was shooting near me,
was shot and he fell to the ground.

After that boy had been killed,
I thought I was going to die.

I saw a woman running toward me.
I thought she was my enemy
so I shot her in the belly
and she fell down.

After I shot her,
I left her
and went to where my colleagues were.
Where I fired on her
is where I left her.

I went to my companions
and we captured the town,
then we looted the town—
bicycles,
clothing, tape-players.
After we looted,
we caught some women—
more than nine women.

After Masiaka,
we walked through Moyamba
until we got back to Base Zero.

Those women, when we brought them,
they were sixteen and seventeen years old.
Papay Konde, who was the initiator at Base Zero,
said he wants them to woo them–
he wants to marry them.
Papay Konde took four of the women
to his house.

While we were at Base Zero,
I saw a lot of big men.

All the Kamajor big men
attended a meeting
in an open-air space.

At the meeting, arms
and ammunition
were given to the commander.
He said the arms and ammunition
were to take to Koribundu.

The commander
who was to lead the group
was called to the meeting-place.
He said Koribundu
is a village where rebels are based.
He said, "So, when you go there,
those that you meet at Koribundu,
they are all rebels.
You should kill all of them
and burn all the houses."
That is what he said at the meeting.

But before Koribundu
we had a mission to Kenema.
When we entered Kenema,
we started searching the houses.
Three of us were searching the houses.
One was there to open the door,
another to shoot under the bed,
and another to shoot through the ceiling.

We killed some policemen under the beds.
I and my companion
held one by his clothes.

We dragged him to the center of a field.
Then we brought a tire
and placed it on the man.
There was a mattress.
We dragged it, and we placed it
on the policeman
and we smeared it with petrol
and we set it on fire.
He was burning when we left.

We started going around
capturing some other people
who were collaborators
and setting them on fire.
A collaborator was someone
who was on the rebels' side.

In Kenema, we had another group,
which was called the Yamorto squad.
Well, Yamorto, it was a group
that was meant to eat
people.
The commander who led that group,
I was with him.

When we entered Kenema,
we searched the houses
one after the other.
In the houses we searched,
we captured people.
When we asked them who they were,
they'd say they were civilians.
We'd tell them it's a lie.

We'd say that they are rebels
or collaborators.

After we said that,
we'd tie them up.
When we caught them,
we would tie them and we'd say
"You were doing business
with the rebels."
They would deny that.
They would say they were just with them
in the town.

We would tie them
with an FM—
an FM is a very small stick
that has a rope attached to it.
The rope is a line
used to hang clothes—
a clothesline.

When we captured them,
we'd put them on the ground.
We'd step on their backs.
Then we'd put their elbows together
behind their backs.
We'd put the FM there
and we'd turn it 'round.
When we'd turn it 'round, they'd shout.
Then we'd ask them to tell us the truth.

Some would tell us
that they were old soldiers.

Some would tell us
they were former police.
Some would tell us
that they were with the rebels
but they'd never carried guns.
They would tell us these things
hoping that we would untie them.

After they answered us,
we would take them to the base,
which was the Yamorto base.
It was in Kenema,
Nyandeyama.

When we took them there,
in most cases
it was to eat them.

When we took them there,
in most cases
it was to eat them.

At the base
in Nyandeyama
there was a tree.
Whenever we'd get a person
that we wanted to eat,
we'd take them
and tie them
to the trunk of that tree.
We used a narrow strip of leather
called a "thong."

There was a commander
named Colonel Biko.
Colonel Biko would come
and give us the order
to tie them to the trunk of the tree.

Our base
was close to a swamp.
There we would take the person
to be killed.
When we'd take him there,
when we reached there,
we'd hold him,
we'd put him on the ground.

From there we'd start to stab him
with a bayonet.
Then he would die.

After he died,
the heart,
the liver
and the other parts
in his stomach—
we'd remove them,
and the legs.

Then we'd find a stick
and put the head on it.
We'd take the stick with the head on it
and we'd place it by the gate.

After that,
we'd heat some water

and remove the body parts
in bits
and place them
in the hot water,
then remove the first skin.

After that, we had some oil.
We'd place the oil over the fire.
After that, those body parts
which had been removed
and the skin
which had been removed as well,
we'd place it in the oil
and we would fry it.
We'd fry it in the oil.
And after that we'd prepare some gravy.
And some people
would eat it
with bread.

By then I was twelve years old.

When I was back at Base Zero
my commander held a meeting in Bo.
He came back from that meeting
and met us at Base Zero
and told us that we should come
to Freetown—
we should come to Freetown and fight.

We waited for two or three days
till a helicopter came.
It landed in the field.
The commander called us

and we entered the chopper.
The helicopter brought us to Freetown.

After we disembarked
some men took down our names
and gave us arms.

We were taken in a vehicle
and we came to Congo Cross.
There was heavy gunfire
between the rebels and the ECOMOG.
So we joined in and started fighting
against the rebels,
alongside ECOMOG.

After Congo Cross
we went to Brookfields Hotel.
We knew Brookfields as a hotel
but the Kamajors said this was our base
so we settled there.
We put up a checkpoint there.
That's where we settled in.
We the fighters were there
along with the commanders.

After the fighting had subsided
we left Brookfields
and we heard that Papay Konde
had initiated some more people
into a secret society called Avondo.
Avondo means that when you go to the warfront,
when you sweat
a special medicine
will enter your body.

That is why they call that society
Avondo.

So, we left along with some other Kamajors
to join that new society.

The place where this society
was initiating
was at Bumpe Tabe.
So we reached that village,
Bumpe Tabe.

After we reached the bush
where the initiation took place
we saw many people
who were new Kamajors—
they had just been initiated.
We were the old Kamajors.

When it was time for them to graduate,
that's the time we went there
and we all graduated.
We were given a certificate.
They placed my photo on it.
I don't know how to read
but I can recognize my photo.

By that time I had turned
thirteen.

After a time
we went to Mamban bridge.
For a while
we were at Mamban.

And then we came
back to Freetown.

At that time
some men told us we should disarm
at Brookfields Hotel.
So my companions and I
disarmed.

Some were twelve years old,
some were thirteen,
some were ten—
those are the ages.

At Brookfields Hotel,
a British man
from the UN mission
for disarmament, demobilization, and reintegration—
we call it "DDR"—
instructed me to hand in my gun.
He asked me where I was born
and I told him
Pendembu village,
in Kailahun.

They asked me about my parents.
I told them that I had been
separated from my parents
for a long, long time
so I didn't know where they were.
Then they asked the DDR
to take me to Kenema
to try to trace
my mother and my father.

Some organizations tried
to find my family
but they did not succeed.

Since the day that I was captured
when I was nine years old
I've never seen my parents
or my sisters—
since that separation
I've never seen them.

They tried
to find my mother and my father
but they did not succeed.

Now I'm learning a trade.

THE GRIEVING FATHER
(TF2-088, CDF Prosecution, November 25, 26, 29, 2004)

I am a teacher.
I've got two wives,
eleven children.
My age is fifty-four.

November,
Nineteen ninety-seven,
I sent my eldest son
and three of my nephews
to bring some cassava
to my village
and retrieve my gun
from where I'd hidden it—
I wanted my son
to fetch my gun.

The Kamajors who had come to us
wanted guns—they had no guns.
One of my brothers
from the same father
had joined the Kamajors
and he was made a battalion commander.
He was the one
who asked me to give him my gun.
That is why
I sent my son.

It was early in the morning,
around five o'clock.
Of the four that I sent—
my three nephews and my son—

I wasn't able
to see all of them again.

It's only one
who I ever saw again . . .

My younger son said, "Father,
the gun that you asked my brother to fetch,
I saw it with the Kamajors
in the court barri."
He was referring to a meeting space
that has a roof and open sides.
That was what made me go
to the court barri,
running.

I and my younger son,
both of us went.
When we reached the court barri,
I saw my gun
and a lot of Kamajors.

When I reached there, I said
to the Chief Kamajor
"This is my gun.
Where is my son
who I sent to get this gun?"

This man—he was the Chief Kamajor
for the whole of Valunia Chiefdom—
his name was James Bundu—
said, "That gun that you sent
your children to collect,

you'll not get it again.
It belongs to us now,
the Kamajors. And in fact
we are going to kill
all four of these boys."

I said, "Why
are you going to kill them?"
They said that I
had not allowed my children
to join the Kamajors.
They said, "There is no-one in this section
who does not join the Kamajors,
and whoever does not join us now
is classified a rebel."

Then the Chief Kamajor,
James Bundu, said,
"Your small boy who is standing there—
this one who has accompanied you to the barri—
we are taking him to the stream
where we've tied your children."

The name of that stream
is Taia River.
It was about three hundred yards
from the court barri.
The Kamajors went with my son.
They would not let me
go there.

The Chief Kamajor,
James Bundu, said,

"We're taking your son—
if you follow us
we will kill you."

My younger son
went to the Taia River
and then
at about six that evening
he returned.

When he returned,
he said, "Father,
did you hear
four gunshots?"

I said, "Yes."

He said the first gunshot
was fired by Sundifu Samuka.
He said, "He was the one
who killed my brother."

He said the second gunshot
was fired by Joseph Kulagbanda.
He said he was the one
who fired on my elder nephew.

The third gunshot
was fired by Wan Mohammed.
He was the one who shot
my other nephew.

The three had died
and were thrown into the river.

They killed all three at that same spot.
The Taia River.

My younger son said
at the fourth gunshot—
that final shot—
my small nephew ran away
downriver.
He was trying to cross.

As he tried to cross
they shot him in the back.
Then he sank into the water,
but my younger son did not know
whether he'd survived.

Later that night,
around nine P.M.,
I was in my bedroom
and I heard talking
on the veranda.

A group of Kamajors
were there on the veranda.
They said, "that teacher's son,
he did not die.
He did not die.
A group of Kamajors
came to that village
and they have taken him
to Mandu."

I heard that. I said, "Oh."
Then I started praying to God.

So early the next morning
I woke one of my children
and I said, "I'll go to Mandu.
I heard that my smaller nephew
did not die."

We went on foot.
We went there,
seven miles.
It took two hours.

I went to the base
of the other Kamajor battalion,
at Brima Sheki's compound.
All of them were there.

I saw my nephew and his mother—
her name was Jeneba—
standing amidst the Kamajors
and a large group of civilians.
Jeneba was my niece—
my sister's daughter.
My nephew was Jeneba's child.

My nephew was weak.
He had no clothes on.
As I was looking at my nephew and his mother,
James Bundu and the other four
Kamajors
alighted from a vehicle
and came to the compound
where we were.

They called the battalion commander
and they all entered the parlor.
They were in the parlor,
then they came out.

The Chief Kamajor said
"You, Jeneba, you were the town mother."

Jeneba replied, "I was captured by the rebels.
They said if I escaped from them,
they'd kill me. They ordered me
to cook for them. On account of that,
they made me the town mother."

Then the Chief Kamajor said
they would kill her for that
because, they said, she had
cooked for the rebels.
They said they would kill Jeneba.
They would kill her because
she had joined the rebels,
because she was
town mother.

They said they would kill her.

Her daughter was there
and they asked Jeneba
to bid farewell to her daughter.

They asked her to tell her daughter
goodbye.

They took Jeneba
under a mango tree.
Joseph Kulagbanda
and Sundifu Samuka.
They called Philip Mboma
to shoot her.
He was another battalion commander
based at Mandu.
And Philip Mboma shot her.

When he shot her,
she did not fall down.
She said, "Hey, you have killed me."

He took a machete,
and he cut her neck
on the side.
She fell down on the ground
and died.

Then the Chief Kamajor
came to my nephew,
and asked, "Were you the one
that was shot at yesterday
who did not die?
Now, you're going to die."

The same James Bundu said,
"The rebel king of Valunia Chiefdom
was sending you to go catch fish for him.
So you, too, are part of the rebels.
Now we're going to kill you."

So they held my nephew by his hands
and his two feet.
They took him and placed him
over the corpse
of his mother,
Jeneba.

The same Philip Mboma
who had just killed Jeneba
brought a long machete
and cut my nephew in two.

When he was cut,
his head went one way
and his feet went the other way.

When he was cut in two,
he was bowed down on the ground.
All the intestines came out.
One part went this way
and the other part, the other way.

Yes, he died.

. . .

My other child was called.
They called my other child,
with whom I had gone to Mandu.
This now was Gibril Mansaray,
the clerk of the Kamajors.

They said, "You and another four civilians
are to go and dig a grave

for the people we have killed.
You will dig a hole to bury them."

They went and dug a grave.
I saw them come
and take Jeneba away.

Two of the five
who had dug the grave
came and held Jeneba by the hand,
dragged her along by the hand,
till they took her away.

They took her toward the place
where they had dug the grave,
but I didn't go there.
My son stayed at the graveside
with two others.

The two civilians who had taken Jeneba away
came back to bury my nephew.
They protested that my nephew
had only sheets on him.
So the Kamajors told them
to remove the clothing
that had been on his mother,
so they could wrap it 'round the boy.

They went and brought his mother's dress
and they took the two parts
of his body
and put the two parts in that dress
and took the two parts of his body
away.

They killed them there
and they buried them there
in Mandu.

I stayed in Mandu
from nine A.M.
till one in the afternoon.
At one, my child came
and told me, "Papa,
we've buried the bodies."
Straightaway we moved
and returned to my home.

At seven that night,
James Bundu
sent John Rainbo—
another Kamajor commander—
to bring me to the court barri.

When I reached the court barri,
I saw many commanders
and other Kamajors.
James Bundu asked me, "Were you the one
who called us 'cannibals'?"

When he asked me,
I stood for a while.
I did not want to answer.
And they said if I didn't answer
they would give me FM.
Then I said, "Yes, I said it."

They said, "We'll show you
what cannibalism is.

We'll show you
that we are cannibals now."

I was grabbed by my feet
and placed on the ground.
They stripped me naked.
They tore my trousers.
I didn't have anything on my body.

They called for an FM
and they brought it.
My hands were placed behind my back
and they tied me with that FM rope.

Then James Bundu brought a lot of charcoal
and the charcoal was broken by stone
on the cement.
The charcoal was ground
to a fine beat.
They brought some white clay
from a fireplace
and mixed it in with the charcoal.
They added water to it.
They started to paint
my body with this.
They smeared it on my body.

Then they brought pepper.
They put it in a tin metal cup
and rubbed it on my penis.
They said it's Vaseline.

I lay down there for a while
and they told me that they wanted

to release me
but that I should pay five thousand leones.

Before I paid, I asked them to bring
the shirt that they had removed from me.
There was money in the shirt,
forty-one thousand leones.

They started asking each other,
"Who took his shirt? Who took his shirt?"
Then I said, "Yes, I know,
it's James Bundu
who took my shirt."

So James Bundu called
one of his bodyguards—
he had a bodyguard
who brought the shirt
and gave it to him.

I told them to open the chest pocket—
"There is money there,
forty-one thousand leones."
I asked them to take the five thousand leones
and return the difference to me.

When they opened the pocket,
they saw an envelope,
and they said
it's only an envelope.
Then I told them
to open the envelope.
They opened it and they saw the sum
of forty-one thousand leones.

James Bundu stepped on my stomach
and said that the money wasn't mine,
that I came here without any shirt on.
So I told him that I couldn't be
walking around without any clothes
on my body. I told him, "It's my shirt."
He said, "No, you're not the owner.
In fact, you're not the owner of this money."
They didn't give it to me.
They said it's not mine.

They called about thirteen commanders,
and told them to form a line.

James Bundu said, "This man
has called me a thief,
because that money that was in that pocket,
he laid claims to, so he has told lies.
So each one of you should give him
ten lashes."

Each one of them beat me ten.
Someone would come—one,
two, three, four,
five, six, seven,
on different parts of my body.
Each one of them,
ten lashes.

I was almost going to die
and if I shook at all,
they beat me more.

After they beat me,
a woman came and said,
"This is my sister's husband.
I volunteer to pay that money,
that five thousand leones
for his release."
And they said, "Pay, pay."

And the woman took the cloth
that was wrapped around her waist—
we call it "lappa"—
and she let them hold that garment
while she went to collect the money
from her house.
She came and paid
the five thousand leones
and the lappa was returned to her.

Then they asked her to bring a razor blade
to remove the rope
that had broken my skin.
So she brought the blade
and they cut the rope
that had broken my skin.

The scars are here
where they wounded me—
Look, sir,
there are many scars.

They released me and I went
to my house.

. . .

Almost one and a half years
later,
on the twenty-second of April,
Nineteen-ninety-nine
I left my village
to walk to a nearby village
to ask my sister
for three penny pans of rice.
I was there for one hour,
then I set off for home.

As I was on my way home,
I heard my child scream,
my younger son,
the same one with whom
I had left Mandu.

I heard him scream
"Leave me, leave me,
I didn't steal that chicken.
It was given to me by my sister.
I didn't steal it."

He was born when I was twenty-three
so I know his voice.
I know his voice.
I knew it was my son.

I was within fifty yards
of where the boy
was screaming,
and I pointed a flashlight
toward that end.

He was in the hands
of the Kamajors.
They had captured him
and he was shouting, "Leave me,
leave me. I didn't steal that chicken.
It was given to me by my sister."

I saw a bunch of Kamajors
and they said, "Turn off your flashlight."
I turned it off.

When I turned it off,
I heard a gunshot—
an explosion: Boom.

A gunshot.
Boom.

A gunshot.

I also heard
one of my former students—
Borbor Aruna—
say, "He has not died properly.
Give me the machete,
give me that machete.
It is sharper. Let me cut him."

Borbor Aruna said, "He's not dead
yet. You, Mr. Robin,
you don't know how to shoot properly.
You should have shot him in his head.
You didn't shoot him properly.
You, Mr Robin.

Let me cut his throat.
He's not yet dead."

So he cut my son's throat.
My son, who was screaming.

Then Mr. Robin,
who had shot the boy,
called me,
"Teacher, come and pass now."
I didn't say a word.
I just stood still.

I pointed the flashlight
and I saw my son's throat cut,
bleeding.
I saw him bleeding and gasping.

I pointed the flashlight there
for about three minutes.
Then I ran away.
I went back to my village
that very night.

Early the next morning,
my daughter's boyfriend
came from Bo.
He said, "Teacher,
there was jubilation
at Gumahun
yesterday.
I wanted to come to you
last night,
but they told me not to come.

Something was happening
in your village,
so they kept me in Gumahun."

Late in the night, he said,
around ten P.M.,
there was a lot of jubilation
that they have killed my son.

And the ashes
of the child,
he said,
were going to be used
to initiate Kamajors.

The marks that are put
on the body of each initiate
must be from human ash—
it is human ash
that is put on it.

Early in the morning
I came back to that spot
with three of my nephews
and my daughter's boyfriend
who had come from Bo
and we saw my son.

We turned him around
in the place where they had shot him
and we saw where his throat
had been cut.

Then we saw a group of people
coming toward us
and we heard the voices
of Kamajors,
so we ran away.

I knew their voices
because they're my brothers,
we're from the same village,
and I said, "They are coming.
I'm afraid of them."

So we ran to the swamp,
about one hundred and twenty yards
from where the boy was.

We stood under a tree
known as a "Wanda tree."
We stood there, looking in the direction
from where the Kamajors approached.

We saw Chief Mulai
and David Joseph, the camp commander
and his assistant, Borbor Aruna
and Eddy Sorboi.

Eddy Sorboi came to where we were
and he saw me
and he sat on the roadside.

At the spot where we had seen
the boy's body,
Chief Mulai and David Joseph

from Gumahun—
they went there.

They were there
for over thirty minutes,
then they left.

As they were leaving,
I saw a polyethylene
plastic bag, a black one,
which was carried by Aruna.

Chief Mulai was in front,
Aruna in the middle,
David Joseph in the rear.
They departed, and headed toward
the town from whence they'd come—
Nyandehun.
Eddy Sorboi followed them.

My daughter's boyfriend
who had come from Bo
said, "they must have done something there.
Let's go there."
So we went.

When we got there
we found that they had opened my son's stomach
up to the throat,
from his penis
up to his throat,
closer to his throat,
wide—
they had opened widely.

His abdomen had been removed
up to his ribs.
His heart was not there.
His lungs were not there.

His intestine was cut into bits.
And the oily liquid
that had been within it
still dripped on the leaves.
They had drawn out
his intestine.
Some parts were longer, some four yards,
some one foot.
It was cut in bits.
There was no more oil in it.
They had removed the oil.
It was cut in bits.

We left his body there.

The Kamajor rule
was that if they killed someone,
no civilian has the right
to remove the body,
and if you do
then you too will be killed.
It had happened
to other people
and I had seen that,
so we left his body there.

He was killed
on the twenty-second of April.
His belly was opened

on the twenty-third,
and on the twenty-fourth,
they came and said
they were going
to burn his body.

I knew because I saw a letter
at Grima checkpoint,
which had been written
by the Kamajor clerk.

The letter read: "Please, checkpoint commanders,
we saw a chicken with—"
The letter was about that,
about the chicken that had been
with my son.

It was an order
that my son
should be killed
immediately.

And that the ashes
should be used
to do the last initiation
in Mongeray town.

That was the content of the letter I saw
at Grima checkpoint,
that my son should be killed
because he stole a chicken.
That was the content of the letter.

The letter was shown to me
by Gibril.
He was the checkpoint commander
at Gumahun.

Two days later
the checkpoint commanders
and other Kamajors
burned my son's body
in a valley.
We looked on.

I went up a hill
about one hundred and twenty yards
from that valley.
I lay on top of a stone.

After he was burned,
the ringleaders
and a bunch of other Kamajors
came to my village.
It was about five-thirty
P.M.

They said, "No-one
will sleep in this village.
Everyone move out!"
They started beating my children.
They started beating them.

They said, "You have to feed us today."
They took everything we had.
I'm a teacher,
and at that time

the government had paid me
three months' salary—
they took that money.
They drove us
from our home.

We left at night.
Twenty-five of us.
Then these Kamajors
burned down my house.

We made a report
that very night,
after we were driven out.
We went three miles,
to Bo.

We went to the battalion commander.
I told him
"Your Kamajors have killed my child.
They have taken all my property.
They have burned my house.
They have said I have to feed them.
They have taken everything from me
and driven us from our home.
That is what they have done."

. . .

The battalion commander said,
"There is a ceasefire.
The police are now in their various stations.
We were ordered
not to kill anyone anymore.

Even if a rebel is captured,
we should take him to the police.
And what was done to you
we didn't know about
so I will send some people
to go investigate."

So in the morning
twenty-fifth of April
Nineteen ninety-nine
three Kamajors—these were
the delegates whom he had sent—
came to my village
and we went to the spot
where my son had been burned.

When we got to where he was burned,
the wood that they'd brought,
we saw it
where it had been thrown
to the side
along with some charcoal
and three stones.
We found the ashes
and a lot of charcoal.

The investigators went around the area
and a man wrote down
what they had found.
I was with the man
until he finished writing.

Then we came back to my compound
in my village.
They went into all of the rooms.

I had a poultry farm,
I had a lot of chickens.
When we came
with the investigators,
we only saw the feathers
and entrails.

I told these men,
"I left over one hundred chickens.
When we were driven out yesterday,
we left everything behind."

I told them, "You see these huts?
This is where my chickens were.
They have taken all of them."
And I had eggs,
more than fifty eggs,
we didn't even see any of those.

The investigator said,
"I have seen the feathers.
There are so many."

He asked if there was any other thing.
I said that I didn't even see the pots,
and I didn't even see the dishes.
Five bags of rice were gone.
Even my clothes were not in the room.

The investigator wrote all of this down.
He collected some specimens
of the feathers.

Two days after the investigators left,
a Kamajor came to me
and said that I was needed
in Gumahun
urgently.
So I went there,
to the court barri.

There, the assistant battalion commander
asked me, "Are you the one
who reported to the battalion commander
that they've killed your son,
that they've taken his parts
and burned them?"

He asked, "Are you the one
who said they looted your home
and took all your property away?"

I said "Yes, I am."

He said, "I was sent
in relation to this case.
That is why I am here.
The chief battalion commander
has asked me to come
and look into this case."

He went on,
"Have you seen all these Kamajors

who have come here?
Have you seen all these Kamajors
in their numbers?"

He said, "Concerning the report which you made,
I was asked to invite all these people
whose names you have mentioned."
He asked if I knew these people
he'd brought,
the ones whose names
I had mentioned.

He said: "The report which you made,
who are the main leaders?"
He asked me this question.
And I named them.

I said, "These people, they killed my child,
they took his parts,
they burned them,
and they drove me from my village
in the night."

He asked them whether what I have said is true.

At first they denied,
but later they answered.
They said "Yes, we killed him.
We burned him.
We drove them out of their village."

This meeting went from noon
till five P.M.
At the end, the investigator said

that I should itemize all the things
that they had taken away from me.

They calculated the value.
The clerks were there,
and a pastor, Joseph Earnest.
He did the counting.
The amount
went up to two million leones.
The investigator said they would pay
for all that they had taken away.

He said, "Now this man has said
that for two days now
he has been living on wild yams
in the bush.
He has no pepper and no salt.
So give him something today
that he can use to feed his family."

They went and brought
twenty thousand leones
and five gallons of oil,
and they gave that to me.

He told them, "The amount that is owed
is a lot.
Therefore, every two weeks
give the teacher
five hundred thousand leones
until the full amount is paid."

But they never did.

THE RAPE SURVIVOR
(TF1-305, RUF Prosecution, July 27, 2004)

I'm not married.
I have no children.
I never went to school.

I speak two languages:
Kono and Krio.
I went to a training institute
where I learned the tailoring trade.
Kono is my home.

I've also lived in another town,
called Bumpeh.
I lived with my elder sister in Bumpeh.
I spent a long time there.

The time I was there,
something happened,
which I am able to explain to this Court.

The things I remember,
can I explain them now?

There came a time
when I heard there were elections.
They said there was one candidate
whose name was Kabbah.
That was the first I'd heard
about someone called Kabbah
who was standing in the elections.
After the elections,
I heard that Kabbah had won.

I spent a long time in Bumpeh,
then I moved from Bumpeh
and I went to my own town
where I was born,
where my mother lived.
That's where I was with my mother.

At that time things happened.
Yes, I am able to tell the Court.

There came a time
that we had celebrations of Christmas
in the town.
We had celebrations of the New Year
in our town.

Two weeks after the New Year's celebrations
we were in our town
and we heard gunfire.
When we heard the gunfire,
everybody in the town panicked.
Everybody just took his or her luggage
and fled.
I escaped with my mother, my father,
and one old woman.

While we were running,
this old woman followed us.
We arrived in the forest.
We arrived in the bush.

When we arrived in the bush,
my father built a small hut.
That's where the four of us were.

I was with my father, my mother
and the old woman.

We were in the bush for two weeks
when a large group of people arrived
and they were all wearing combat fatigues.
They identified themselves to us.
There were ten of them.
They all had weapons,
they all had guns.

When they came,
they arrested us
and they gathered us in one place.
They said: "Have you ever seen a rebel?"
They asked me whether I had ever seen a rebel
one day in my life.

I said, "No, I have never known
a rebel in my life."
At that time they told us,
"Well, we are rebels at this moment;
we are the rebels at this moment."

They said, "We are in charge of the government.
We own the government now."
They said: "Bring out all your luggage; whatever you have
that is your property, bring it out."
They searched through our luggage
and questioned us.

The four of us: myself,
my mother, my father
and the old woman.

They asked us whether we had any
Kamajors around us. They also said,
"Are there any soldiers here?"
They said: "Do you have guns here?"
"The marijuana that you have,
please bring it out."

We told them, "What you are asking about,
we haven't got."
They went inside the hut,
brought out the bags
that contained our clothes.
They took the best of our clothes from the bags.

They brought everything outside
and they said to my mother:
"We will kill your daughter
or take her away or rape her. Which do you choose?
Which do you want?"

We will kill your daughter
or take her away
or rape her.
Which do you choose?

My mother pleaded with them,
she said: "Look, all these things
you are asking me to choose from,
I'm begging you not to do any of them
to my child.
She's the only young one here."

My mother pleaded
but they didn't listen.
They seized me.

Eight of them took me behind the hut.
My parents were on one side of the hut,
and the eight rebels brought me
to the opposite side
of the same hut.

When they took me
to the other side of the hut,
they told me to undress,
to take off all my clothes.

They told me to lie down.
Each one of them took turns
raping me.
I could just lie there
and I saw one of them come and take his clothes off
and make sex to me.

. . .

Eight of them raped me.
They just told me to lie down
and they were going to make sex to me.

The other two rebels
were guarding my mother, the old woman,
and my father.

After I was raped,
I didn't have much feeling.
I was dazed.

After all these guys had made sex to me,
I just was lying there
as if I was in the hands of death itself.
I was bleeding profusely.

I just lay there
as if in the hands of
death itself.
I was bleeding profusely.

I was scared.
I thought I'd be killed.
They all had weapons.
They all had guns.

At that time I didn't know my age,
my mother had never told me how old I was.
But it was the time when I had come
from the initiation in the woods.
And our people don't do the initiation by years since birth,
they only look at your growth.
When your breasts are full they say,
"This is big enough. Let's put her into the secret society."
At the time this happened,
I had just come from the secluded forest site
where I had been initiated into the Society
as is our custom for girls when they mature.

While they were raping me
I was listening
and I heard them call themselves
various names.

The commander who was the big man
and had the bigger gun
called the others
Killer, Copul, RUF, and Liberia Boy.
These are the names that he called them.

They spoke two languages.
They used Krio
and they used English with a Liberian accent.
The way they were speaking
and the name that their boss called one of them
suggested to me there were Liberians among them.

After they raped me,
they said, "Let's go."
But before they left, they said
"We are leaving you behind.
If you run away
from where we are now leaving you
and we find you at any other place,
we will kill you.
You must stay here in this one place
both night and day."

When they left us,
they took all our property.
When they left, my mother came
and lifted me up. I couldn't stand.

My mother took me and placed me down
and put a large pot over the fire
to boil some water.
When the water was hot,
she placed it down to cool a bit

and she put some quantity of salt in it
and placed me in it.

Even though I sat in there,
still I kept bleeding.
I bled for three days.

When I stopped bleeding,
at that time I could no longer feel
when I wanted to urinate,
I urinated without even noticing.
The urine leaked out
by itself.
I could no longer feel
the urge to urinate.
The urine leaked out
continuously.

We stayed in the bush for a long time.
Then my father told us to leave that spot
and we looked for a road
and we went as far as where
we found some Kamajors.

These Kamajors were in Kangama
in Kono.
We lived with the Kamajors for some time
until we saw some military men
who came and told us they were "ECOMOG."
I asked them what this means
and they said they're an armed force
of peacekeepers with units from Nigeria
and other countries in West Africa
whose mission was to help defeat the rebels.

They introduced themselves to us.
They said that they are now in charge of Freetown,
they are in Kenema,
they are in Bo,
and they are trying now to settle
in Kono as well.

We stayed in Kangama for a while.
We left when ECOMOG
ensconced itself in my hometown. ˋ

The distance between Kangama
and my hometown
is long, but when the ECOMOG settled
in my hometown,
that's when we left Kangama.

We followed the ECOMOG soldiers
and went up together with them.
We were all living in our village
with the ECOMOG soldiers.

There came a time
when the rebels attacked the ECOMOG.
They fought for long,
but the rebels were in larger number
than the ECOMOG.
The ECOMOG decided to retreat.
While they retreated,
they decided they didn't want to leave
any of the civilians behind.
They took all of us who were civilians
and they pulled out with us
and went with us to Kenema.

There, we were in a camp
for displaced persons.
While we were in the camp,
there came a time when we were told,
"People have come to us."
These folks were from an NGO called "IRC."
They wanted to talk to us.

They held a gathering where they announced
that they would like to see
all those who'd suffered problems
in this war.

At that time I was very, very much ashamed.
I was unable to appear in public
or even speak about what happened to me
to anyone.

My aunt told me not to be ashamed.
She said, "This urine leak
is an illness
which you got not by your own will
but from this war,
so it is good for you to go and tell them:
maybe they'll be able to help you."

They summoned me
and I explained to them
what happened.
After they listened
they went back to the place
from which they'd come.

After some time
I heard that they had come to me.
They were from IRC.
They took me, at that time,
to a hospital that was in the camp for displaced persons.
They started treating me in that hospital.
They gave me injections
and they gave me pills.

After treating me at the hospital
in the camp for displaced persons,
they took me out of there
and brought me to the Kenema government hospital.
I had an operation there in Kenema,
a second operation in Bo,
and a third operation here in Freetown.

I had my first operation in Kenema,
my second operation in Bo,
my third operation in Freetown.

I'm still not well.
From the time these rebels raped me,
I'm still ill
but I can answer questions
and I can speak.

I'm still not well
but I can answer questions

and I can speak.

THE BLINDED FARMER
(TF1-072, AFRC Prosecution, July 1, 2005)

I am fifty-six years old.
I was born in Tombodu,
Kamara chiefdom,
Kono.
I went to school a long time ago,
and I stopped in third grade.

I'm married. One wife.
We had nine children,
eight alive now.
I work in the bush.
I'm a farmer.

In Tombodu,
February
nineteen ninety-eight,
things happened.

Yes, at that time
things happened.

My wife and I
were in Tombodu
with my children.
People came running.
I said, "Why
are they running?"
I told my wife, "When you see
people moving,
you should run."

"When you see people moving
you should run."

Before I finished this thought
a red vehicle arrived.
A large quantity of soldiers
were in that vehicle.

When the vehicle stopped,
one of my friends came
and told me "from that vehicle,
soldiers have alighted
and they are giving money to people."

I said, "I'm not waiting for money."
I told my wife and children, "Let us move."

We didn't wait. We moved
and we went almost as far
as Wordu.
There's a hill on arriving at Wordu
and the hill is called Igbeda.
We heard gunshots there.
The gunshots came from the rear
from where we came,
Tombodu,
so we didn't want to go back.
We decided to continue ahead.
We didn't wait. We continued on
to Wordu.

On arriving at Wordu,
I told my wife, "What I told you earlier
is what is happening. Look,

we still see people running around."
So we moved from Wordu
and went to Gbaima.

It was late in the evening
when we arrived at Gbaima.
I told my wife, "Where we are sitting
is not safe, because I can still see
people trickling by
and they are running away.
Let's not wait,
let's move ahead."

I went to my in-laws' home,
Kobedenja.

From Tombodu
to Wordu
to Gbaima
to Kobedenja.

Tombodu
Wordu
Gbaima
Kobedenja.

We were there
at my in-laws' home
in Kobedenja
for a while.
I don't remember
the exact date,
because when you have a large number
of people and you are

running away
you're always in a hurry.

When you are running away
you're in a hurry.

At Kobedenja,
we had bush yams.
That's what we fed on.
We ate as many bush yams
as there were in our neighborhood
till the bush yams were gone.

Then one of my friends came
and said, "Let's go further into the bush
and look for bush yams."

I told my wife, "We should go,
because we have to go that far and get food
for us and the children."
So we got up. We went.

We went looking for bush yams.
We climbed up a certain hill.
We saw people
dressed in soldier uniforms,
seven of them.
And in front of them,
a man was tied—
he had a rope tied
'round his waist.

The one who was tied
was in front of all the others.

There were seven soldiers
dressed in uniform—
they were behind.
The man who had the rope tied
'round his waist
did not have any soldier uniform.

The rope was held
by one of the soldiers.
All of them were behind this man
and he was in front of them.
They were going towards
where we had come from.

When we met them, they told us—
they told both myself and my friend—
"Stand here"
and we stood.

They asked us
where we were going.
We said, "We're going looking
for bush yams."

"Why are you going looking
for bush yams
when we have arrived in the town
and we have food?
Why did you not ask *us* for food
when we have come here to save you?"

Then one of them noticed
that we wore tattered shorts

and ripped, rubber-soled shoes.
He looked down at my shoes.

He took my shoes off my feet.
First my right foot was removed
out of my shoe and then the other.
He took the laces out of my shoes
and he asked one of his friends to tie me up.

My hands were passed behind me
and were tied with the laces
of my crepe shoes.
My friend was also tied.
They were heading towards
where we had come from
and they told us to go with them
back to Gbaima.
They were taking us back to Gbaima.
These were big people at that time
so we could not refuse them.

It was not a long distance
between where they caught us
and Gbaima.

On arriving at Gbaima
they told us to lie down,
and they took guns
and they gave one of the soldiers a gun.
He took cartridges out,
two cartridges,
and he inserted one of the cartridges
into the gun.
He said, "These people who are lying down,

if any of them try to escape, shoot them."
We were lying there. We didn't say a word.

We stared at each other intermittently.
And the guy who was the guard
came and stood over us.

This was in March.
I can't remember the exact date,
but I do remember the month.
It was in March.
Nineteen ninety-eight.

One of them was left guarding us,
six of them went into the town
with the man who was tied.
We heard gunshots in the town,
and we saw a lot of people running away,
some going into the bush.

We were tied,
so we were just lying there waiting
for an uncertain end.

We lay there waiting
for an uncertain end.

We asked him whether he could not untie us,
because, we told him, "We will not run away."
He said he hasn't been given the command
to untie us, so he can't do it.
Then I told him, I said, "Okay,
we will not say anything.
We will lie here."

We lay there
for a long time
while the other soldiers
were in the town.
Then they sent another soldier to us
and he came.

Still tied, we were brought into the town.
We got there and we started looking around.
All we saw were properties, bags, and bundles.
Properties, bags, and bundles.
We didn't know what was in these bundles.

We were untied. I looked down,
I saw one man in short pants.
I looked at him
and I looked away.
They took the luggage—
the bags and bundles—
and placed them on our heads,
myself and my friend.
And this other man
who was tied with the rope around his waist
was untied.

When he was untied,
he too was given luggage
to carry on his head.

We traveled far.
We arrived back at the place where
we had been captured,
where we had gone looking for yams.

We were now heading towards Tombodu.
We arrived at a particular spot.
We were not yet in Tombodu,
nor were we in Gbaima any more.

We came upon two men
who had also been foraging for food.
The soldiers saw them and asked,
"Where did you come from?"
"We came from looking for food."

One of the soldiers took
the machete he had with him
and struck him on his back.
We couldn't say a word.
He said, "Drop what you are
carrying on your head."
The man set down the sack
that was on his head.

Then the soldier tore the bag open.
All that was in it
were raw bananas
and some kola nuts.

The soldier struck the other man
with the machete
and tore open his sack too:
all it contained
were raw bananas.

The soldier said,
"We are here to save you.

We have settled in Tombodu
and we have food.
Why didn't you come to us?"
He said, "Let's go back."

One of the soldiers
was carrying some luggage
and he placed that luggage
on the heads of these two men.
We started to walk.

We were going towards Tombodu.
We arrived close to Wordu.
We no longer spoke.

When we arrived at Wordu—are you listening?
When we arrived at Wordu,
as we descended,
one of the soldiers left our midst
and ran into a room, into a parlor.

We couldn't look around too much
because they all had guns.
We were afraid.

He entered one of the rooms in the house.
He came out again running.
My friend and I just looked at each other.
The soldier came out running.
He told the others, he said,
"I have finished him. You see the blood
on my machete, I've finished him."
We didn't say a word.

We continued going.
We were now coming towards Tombodu.
As we arrived in Tombodu
we saw a young man
who was likewise approaching Tombodu.
The soldiers had seen him from afar.

One of the soldiers shouted, "Hey you,
where are you going? Come here."
And he came.
"Where are you going?" the soldier asked.
"I'm going to Wordu."
"What's on your head?"
The man replied, "It's palm wine."
The soldier said, "Put it down,"
and the man placed it down
and the palm wine
was seated on the ground.

The soldiers put our luggage down
and we sat on the ground.
They stood over us.
They were our bosses.
They said that they were here to save us.
We didn't have any power.
We said nothing.
We sat on the floor.

They put the palm wine down.
There was a jerry can—
we call it a "five-gallon."
There were two five-gallons
of palm wine.

One of the soldiers
took one of the two cups
that was in the big bowl.
He took one of the cups,
and he poured the palm wine
into the cup.

Another soldier took the other cup
and poured some palm wine into the cup.
They started drinking and sat down.

We were watching them as they drank.
They drank for a while.
One of them left us
and sat apart.
He took something from his pocket,
white paper.
He looked into his other pocket
and pulled out something in a plastic bag.
It was some leafy stuff.
I didn't know what leafy stuff.
He wrapped that leafy stuff
in the paper
and they lit it.
They started smoking.
They smoked for a while.
They smoked in turns.
When the one smoked
he would come back to drink palm wine
and then go back to smoke.

They said, "We are now in a small party,
all of us together."

So they smoked in turns.
One would smoke, come back, drink palm wine,
go back and smoke. We were watching them.

Then we reached the first house in Tombodu,
just across the river on the left-hand side.
We found a soldier there.
He came out and asked, "Where did you come from
with the slaves?"
The other one replied,
"We don't know where
we caught them from,
I don't know the name
of the town."
He said, "These slaves
were wandering in the bush
and we came."

The soldier said, "Look at me.
It is me that they refer to
as Small Mosquito."
He said, "My name
is Small Mosquito."
We said, "Okay."

They said, "We are going to our boss."
We stood in front of them.
We went and arrived at their boss's house.
They said we should sit down.

When we arrived at the compound
they removed the luggage from our head
and they placed it at the center
of the open space.

We looked at the soldiers,
each one with a gun,
all their guns leaning.
We didn't know if they were
having a meeting.
Then one of them rose.

He rose, left the crowd
and stood apart.
That's when I knew
who was the boss.

Then the other one
stomped his foot
and saluted,
he raised his hand
toward the side of his head
and he said,
"Mr. Savage, sir."
He called him Mr. Savage.

Then he told Savage,
"Where you sent us from,
we have arrived.
The luggage here
is what we've brought."

He turned around
and looked at us
and said we should sit down.

We sat on the steps.
Fourteen of us sat on one side.
While we were seated,

I was in front.
Savage came and asked me,
"Where were you? We came here to save you.
Why didn't you come in time?"
We said, "We don't know. We heard gunshots.
We heard jets overhead.
We were afraid,
so we didn't stay in town."

Then I got up,
he slapped me on my back
with a machete
and I shouted.
Everyone was watching.
Savage said,
"You are the people who killed soldiers."

And I said, "We don't kill soldiers.
Ever since I've been born, now I am growing old,
if you see me holding a machete, I am
brushing a bush, to farm.
Myself and my wife, we make potato heaps,
we plant potatoes, we plant cassavas,
we plant various crops.
Do you think I have enough power
myself to kill a soldier?"

He didn't believe me.
He said I've lied.
He hit me on my leg with a machete
and cut me, cut me on the other
leg as well.

He swept me off my feet
and flogged me on my eyes.
He used the flat side of the machete
and slapped me on my face with it.
What I saw was like fire,
I couldn't do anything,
I fell down.
I was wounded.
My right eye, I still can't see.

My eyes were all flogged.
I can't see properly now.

Then I said to Small Mosquito,
"Look at this amount of beating
that I've received,
can't you speak to them?"

He had a gun and they were drinking.
He took his gun and I was standing
complaining to him about my—
I want you
to come closer.
He stuck the bayonet in my side,
this is my side, my left side.
This is the mark. The scar.
Can you see the scar?

. . .

I couldn't say a word.
All my friends were sitting down,
looking at me.

All I thought about was,
maybe this is time for me to die.

The one who stabbed me with the bayonet said
that we should be tied.
These were big men,
they had power at the time.
We were at their mercy.
It was up to them.

They tied us up. They tied me.
They laid us crisscrossed,
they laid one
and crossed the other on top.
That's how they laid us.

Mosquito was standing at a higher ground
and we were lying down on the floor.
He took out his penis
while we were lying down
and pissed on us.

And I said to myself, "This is now the hour.
This is the hour. This is the hour."
He took one mattress out. A local mattress.
It's grass tucked into sacks.

He looked at the sack of mattress.
He said, "Bring the mattress here,"
and they brought the mattress.

While we were lying down tied,
he said let them lay the mattress on top of us.

They laid the mattress on top of us.
He said let them bring fire.

They brought fire. They lit the mattress.
They lit the mattress
while we were lying underneath.

Well, the fire started to blaze
and they were just standing there
looking at us—
Mosquito and the other soldiers.
The fire caught.
What, fourteen of us
are all going to die here under this fire?

They had tied me,
but my rope was loosened
and I started moving.

You can look at my back,
the fire burnt me
on my shoulder.

You want to
come and look at it?

The fire burnt me on my shoulder.
I didn't wait.

The fire was burning us.
So I wriggled myself out.
I said, "Let what happens, happen. I am
not going to lie here and get burned."

I pushed myself out
and I kicked the mattress
and everybody scattered.

I knew that was fearful.
Savage got up.
He came and repeated, "You see, that's what I said.
These are the ones who kill soldiers."
He swept my feet out from under me
and I fell down on the ground.
He struck me on my face.

He wrecked my eyes.
Up till now I can't see very well.
I went to hospitals.
I mean, they're still giving me medication,
but I can't see properly.
I can see with only one eye.
I was badly flogged.
My back, my lower waist—
so much flogging.

Then Savage told the soldiers
to go and look for vehicle tires.
And he repeated
that we are the ones who kill soldiers.
I told him, "I cannot kill a soldier.
I've never touched a gun in my life.
Machete yes, I use
for working in the bush.
I don't touch guns.
I am afraid of guns.
Me kill a soldier?"

Then Savage shouted,
"Commander, take the guns,"
and they shot,
and one of the people fell.

I said to myself,
"This is the moment."

I started going backwards
slowly.
I know Tombodu a little bit.
I started walking backwards.
I got away.

I still can't see properly.
Up to this moment
I can't see very well.
I was badly flogged.

Are you listening?

Here is the scar.

THE WIDOWER

(TF1-217, AFRC Prosecution, October 17, 2005)

I was born
in nineteen fifty-eight.
I was raised in Koidu.

By February of nineteen ninety-eight
disgruntled soldiers had formed a junta
that ruled the country.
We called them "juntas."
They joined with rebels.
The juntas and the rebels
were in control of Koidu Town.
There was no way to flee.

The elders of Koidu Town
held a meeting
where they decided to ask the Kamajors
to come and drive the juntas and the rebels
out of Koidu.
And for this reason
most of the juntas and the rebels ran away.

Those who remained in town
were captured and burned alive,
to our astonishment, in a pot
which the Kamajors had placed
by the big mosque,
the central mosque in Koidu Town.

Near the roundabout, on the main road going down,
a lieutenant came and surrendered himself.
He said he was a government soldier.

I was standing nearby.
To our surprise, the Kamajors captured him
and killed him.
They opened his chest,
removed his heart and liver,
and shared it among themselves—
they chewed it raw.

Meanwhile, the juntas and the rebels
who had run away
were planning an attack.
We didn't know.

On a certain Friday morning
we heard gunshots. So many gunshots
along with the sounds of bombs.
My wife and our three children
and I, and all of us civilians
ran away,
away from Koidu Town.

My three children, my wife, and I
and some other people
settled in one village
about two miles from Koidu Town.

A soldier came to the village.
I quarreled with him about my sister.
The soldier, Lieutenant Jalloh,
saw my sister and he said,
"We are going to take this girl. She is going
to be my wife."
He was about to capture my sister

and take her away,
but I said no.
My sister was sixteen.

And then one day I saw the soldiers
traveling in Land Rovers,
those are open trucks.
Some girls were in these Land Rovers,
about ten girls.
The smallest one was crying.

She was crying.

Not long after,
my sister went down
to go and fetch water
from the hand pump there.
On her return
some soldiers were seated, drinking,
and my sister was passing by
with a bucket of water on her head
when Captain Bai Bureh
captured her
and said, "She is my wife now.
She is my wife."

I went there to plead,
but he said my life
or my sister—
which do I choose?

If I had spoken
they would have killed me.
So I retreated.

After that, we left that village
and we hid in the forest,
we built huts there.
We were in the forest,
on top of a hill
overlooking the town.

One day we heard a radio
announcer say that ECOMOG
had taken over Koidu Town.
So we packed up our luggage in joy
and we headed for Koidu Town.
We walked for four whole days.

After we walked for those four days
I got tired. So we rested
in a town that had been burned
where there were corpses all around.
We sat down there.
We were resting,
waiting for day to break
so that we could enter Koidu Town
at dawn.

After about an hour,
we saw some people running towards us,
I saw an old man
whose shoulder was oozing blood.
He said he had been shot.
They told us that it was not ECOMOG
in Koidu Town.
They said it was not ECOMOG:
it was the juntas and the rebels.

We were scared.
We took up our belongings.
This was a mining area
and I knew the area a bit
from mining there
so I led the way.
We took the bush path—
my three children, my wife, and I
and some of the others who were with us.
We were afraid that the juntas and the rebels
might chase the people
who had run away from the town—
that's why we left that place.

In the morning we sat down
under a certain mango tree.
I told my wife to prepare food
because we had pots and some rice.
As my wife was preparing this food,
I was about to climb the mango tree,
because in April the mangoes
in Kono
had gotten ripe.
My daughter warned me not to climb,
she was afraid that I'd fall down.
So I descended, and my daughter
shook the mango tree
and the ripe ones dropped.

She came down and sat by me.
I was hungry
and the children were hungry as well.
I was trying to learn
whether my wife had prepared the food.

It was then we heard gunshots,
heavy, heavy gunfire
in the town, in Penduma.
I saw those who were trying to flee.
The soldiers were shooting them down.

My children came close to me,
under the mango tree.
We sat down under the mango tree
and we and the other civilians
were all captured,
those of us who didn't die.

Then the soldiers took
the pregnant women,
the children,
and the suckling mothers aside.
They were all in one place.
My children were among them.

All the women who were not pregnant
or suckling mothers
were placed off to another side—
my wife among them.

We men
were divided into three rows.

Not long after that, I saw Staff Alhaji come—
Alhaji Bayoh—
He had a staff in his hand.
When he'd wield that staff,
the soldiers knew what he meant.

I didn't know what he had whispered
to some of his men who were near him.

Then Staff Alhaji said that the first row of men
should be tied,
and the soldiers tied them up.
These men were taken to a house,
they were placed inside the house,
the house was locked
and the house was set on fire.
The people inside were crying.

The people were crying.

It took some time,
then the crying died down,
we saw the flames.
I knew those people
had been burnt alive—
we saw the fire
and we heard the screams.
We heard the screams.
Then the soldiers came back.

Staff Alhaji turned
to the next group of men
and pointed at that group.
One boy brought a bag
and overturned it
and some knives dropped on the ground.
Alhaji took those knives
and said, "You guys know what to do"—
the soldiers picked up the knives,

brought the group of men
to the area behind the school
and slit their throats.

The reason I came to know
their throats were slit
was that later on
I passed behind that place
and I saw what had happened
to those men.

But two of these men
tried to escape.
Those two were shot.
They were trying to run away.

Our own line,
nothing was done to our line
in the interim.

Then Staff Alhaji told his boys
that the pregnant women,
the children, and the suckling mothers
should go free.
And so they were set free.

My children did not flee
because I was still in that other line.
So they stayed there, waiting.

Then Staff Alhaji pointed to the women.
And some of Staff Alhaji's boys
pounced on the women
and started raping them.

They raped them in full view,
including my wife.
Staff Alhaji told me, "You watch
what they be doing to your wife."

She was raped by eight men.
They pounced on my wife.
I tried to plead but in vain.

Eight of them raped her in my view,
in full view of the group of children
including my own children
and in full view of the group of men.

Six women were killed there,
including my wife.
Junior killed my wife.
Stabbed, she was stabbed.
My children were sitting nearby,
watching.

After they raped my wife,
Tamba Joe—they called him T-Joe—
he was a government soldier—
held my wife
while Junior killed her.

Later,
Staff Alhaji told me
I should go.
So I got up to go.

I heard him tell my children,
"Follow your father."

I turned my back to go.

My children followed me.

THE GRAVEDIGGER
(TF1-253, AFRC Prosecution, April 15, 18, 19, 2005)

April, nineteen ninety-nine:
I remember.
I know what happened.
I never forget anything.
I will answer.

You want to know
what happened in our town?

One morning, a Friday,
we saw some people
in our town.
They came from a village
called Ro-Taron.

They made a complaint
to the soldiers and the Gbethis—
Gbethis were militias
under the CDF umbrella.
The villagers told the soldiers and the Gbethis
that their people at Ro-Taron
had been killed by rebels.
They made a plea
that they needed help
to bury them.

The Gbethis and the soldiers
summoned us.
They called some young men
and said to go and dig

so that the people killed by rebels
could be buried.

I was among those selected to go.
They gave me a shovel.
I held it.
We were about to leave
for Ro-Taron.
We started,
but we never reached there.

As we were going,
we walked in a line.
The Gbethis were leading us.
They were in front.
We, the civilians, were behind.

We were on our way.
We heard a gunshot.
We heard sporadic firing.

The Gbethis told us
that we should run away,
that we'd been targeted by rebels.

We ran away.
We returned to the village
we had come from.

As we arrived there,
we were being pursued.
The Gbethis and the rebels
were shooting at each other
so I went past that spot.

I ran into the bush and I took my wife:
we fled.

We went to another village
called Ro-Konta
two miles away.
I had my business there.
I had my mother there.
I had some of my children there.

When I reached Ro-Konta,
I told my mother that we had to go
because there was a lot of shooting
nearby, the rebels were not far.
So my mother, my wife, my children and I
went on to Lungi.

I took my cigarettes
and my diamonds
that we were selling
and I told my brothers
that we had to flee.

We followed a path,
which is a shortcut
that led us to another
town, Port Loko.

I gave my brothers
the cigarettes
to carry on their heads
in jerry cans.

Well, as we were going,
as we approached the town,
a town called Makambisa,
just by the forest
that was near the town
we came to know
we had been drawn
right into where the rebels were.
We had not known before.

Behind us, we saw some
pointing their guns
and they said, "Wait."
We waited.
We wanted to run,
but we couldn't advance
because others
had come right in front.

Thus they captured us.
They took our cigarettes,
stripped off my timepiece.
I had some money in my bag,
they took the money away from me.

The two that captured me,
one had a combat uniform.
The other wore civilian clothes.
That one asked me
whether I knew him.
I told him I did not.

He said he was one of the rebels.
He said he was part of the group

that was led by "Superman."
There were some branches
that had been formed into a bench
under a tree.
And something happened there.

When they took us there
they asked my younger brother
if he was a Gbethi.
The child said he wasn't a Gbethi.
They asked my other little brother.
They asked him if he was a Gbethi.
This fellow was a stammerer.
He wasn't able to give
a quick reply.

They shot him and they said he was a Gbethi,
that he was trying to be proud.
The child fell.

So of the three of us that were together,
they shot one and he fell.
And then the other brother, too,
was shot in the head
and he fell down.

Then there I was.
They took my hands right at the back
and tied me on the elbows.
And they tied my legs
at the knees.
They passed the rope
around my waist.
I fell down on my shoulder.

My head wasn't able
to touch the ground.

They brought two of my other brothers
and my stepmother.
That makes three.
One of the rebels stood up
and hacked one of my brothers
on the head. The child said,
"Oh, my brother, they are killing me."
Then they shot him
and he fell.

My stepmother, they took her
and they said they were going to rape her.
One of them said, "I'll take her,"
and the other said, "*I'll* take her."
And they brought her behind a house.

After they brought her there
some minutes passed
and before they came back
I heard a gunshot.
And they did not return with her.

The third one with me
was a child. They asked me about him.
I explained that he'd been raised in Freetown.
They said they would not kill him.
They said that he would be with them.
The child sat on their laps.

Then, from where I was seated
I saw them bring one of my sisters

with her children.
She was pregnant.
I saw her mouth had been split open
at the jaw.

She had two children—
one was strapped to her back.
The other she was holding by the hand.

The one strapped to her back
was nearly three years old.
The one whose hand she held
was four.

When she was brought,
one rebel shot
the baby girl
strapped on her back.
My sister too was shot.
Both child and mother
fell together.

Both of them fell together.
Neither one
got up again.

He snatched the other child—
her son, who had been
holding his mother's hand—
and struck him on the neck
with a stick.
That was the child who had been
holding my sister's hand.

They struck him and he fell
and he died there.

. . .

Well, when you see me crying it's because
I'm thinking about my brothers
and my sister.

After they had killed my sister
and her daughter
and her son,
where my sister was lying down
they cut off her leg
on the right thigh.
After she was killed,
they cut off her leg
at the thigh.

My little brothers who had been shot
and killed before my sister and her children—
they lay there. They were shaking their toes.

What—what—what led me to say
they were shaking their toes
is that the rebels realized
they had not yet died
so they cut off their feet.

After that, one of them came
and struck me with the butt of the gun.
He injured me on my head.

Then they extinguished
a marijuana cigarette
on the skin of my leg.

While I was lying down
I was feeling the pain
where I was tied.
They said they were going to take me to Manarma
to their big men.
It's around two miles.
Two of them took me there.

When we approached the bridge,
we met some rebels bathing.
Some were in uniforms. Some wore civilian clothes.
They said I was a Gbethi.
They started slapping me.
Some struck me on my back.

I told them that I was not a Gbethi.
Those who had captured me
said nothing should be done to me.
They had to take me to the big men.

We went to the town.
When I entered the town,
I saw something
and I felt very, very sorrowful.

I felt so filled with sorrow.

As I approached the town,
I saw a woman lying down.
They had already severed her head.

She had been pregnant.
And from this pit in her stomach, on the side
the baby's hand protruded.

When we arrived in town,
the big men I was taken to—
one was Colonel Sesay.
The other one was Johnson.
Johnson was fat.
His hair was plaited.

Colonel Sesay wore combat dress.
He had a cap on.
The cap was cut. This cap,
the spaces for the eyes were cut out
and the mouth was too
so that the eyes and mouth
could be seen through the cut.
It's very rare to see that sort of cap.

Colonel Sesay was fair in complexion.
He was not that tall.
He wore a uniform.
He was a little bit fatter than I am.

They asked me if I was a Gbethi.
I answered I was not a Gbethi.
They told me to sit down on the ground.
While I was seated there
I saw this Johnson speak
into this thing they call a solar,
it is a satphone that gets power
from the sun.

There I heard Johnson talk.
And Colonel Sesay too
spoke on that phone.
He called some names of towns.
I heard him say
that they had captured Manarma,
and Makambisa
and that they were on
"Operation No Living Thing."

Operation No Living Thing.

And so now all
was under their control.
That's what I heard him saying
on the phone.

From where I sat
I could see some houses in the town,
especially one house
that was across from us.

From inside a room
I heard a lot of voices
crying, saying, "We want water.
Please give us some water to drink."

I saw five other people brought
to this same house.
The men who brought them there
were holding guns.
One of them opened the door,
and they pushed these people
into the room.

Then they got a padlock
and locked them in.
I saw they took some nails
and nailed the window shut.

I was still seated
near where the bosses were.
It was then that Johnson came
and said they wanted to go.
He said I should show them where to pass.
I showed them a road.

That road passed through a town
called Robobara
where Nigerian soldiers
were fighting them. So Johnson said
I was a liar and I should be killed.
Johnson said I should be killed.

So the fellow drew the cord
that was tied around my waist,
and I fell on the other side of the veranda.

Then Colonel Sesay said,
"this one, let us not kill him.
Let's leave him now.
Let us not kill this man."

He said to me that I should be with them.
I should carry their loot.
And if I tried to run away
if I was caught
I would be skinned alive.
I said, "Well, I won't run away."

Then the one who held the cord
that was tied around
my waist—it was a cable
that was tied right around my waist,
just like you do to animals—
he held the other end of the rope
and he led me. And I went
and sat where I had sat before,
where the big men also sat.

By then it was going towards evening.
I was sitting near
some rubber containers.
The kind that are used to store
palm oil.

While I was seated there
I saw a man take one of those containers—
it was not properly caulked.
And what was inside spilled
and when it spilled
that was the time I knew
that it was filled
with petrol.

I saw him transfer the petrol
to a smaller jerry can—
it was small
but still at least a gallon.
By this time
night had fallen.

I saw the house
these people had been locked within.

For us, the houses in the provinces
are made of palm leaves.
All these leaves were on top of the house.

I saw this man sprinkle the petrol
on top of the house.
Then they struck a match
and threw the match
onto the leaves.
The roof caught fire.
The people started screaming.

No-one came out of that house.

There was no possibility
of leaving that house:
the door was padlocked
from the outside,
the window was nailed shut.

Then the big man said
that they should move
and go to Bakay
at Port Loko.

We headed for Port Loko.
I was on a cord.
They walked with me
just like you walk a goat.

They said that we were going to fight.
It's more than five miles. It's a little bit far.
We arrived at Port Loko late at night.
We approached a house.

One of the men
among the group that held me
was called Born Naked.
He went into the town
to view the situation
and buy some cigarettes.

Born Naked came back from the town
and gave some information—
he told the big men that
Malian forces from the ECOMOG
were now at Schlenker
and they should start to shoot.

When the big men gave the order
the men began to fire.
Those with whom I was—
Colonel Sesay's boys—
they started shooting as
they came into the town.

The firing at that time
was terrible
and I was panic-stricken.
I was with the man who held the cord
with which I was tied.
I could not just walk alone.
They had to walk with me.

The shooting went on for a long, long time.
I heard a vehicle. I heard it first.
Then the one who held me
informed the big men.
He said the gun that is known as the shaker bomb

is firing now. It's owned by Malian soldiers
who are with ECOMOG. He dropped the cord
that had been tied around my waist.

I ran away. I went to a place
where there were big rocks.
As the firing continued, I hid myself.
I hid between the rocks
because I knew the terrain.

I remained between those rocks
till dawn. Then I crossed over
to a town called Rogbonkom.

When I arrived there
someone gave me
a pair of trousers to put on.

Then they took me to the Nigerian base.
And the Nigerians poured
some medication on the sore
that was on my head.
They gave me an injection
to cure me where I had been tied
so that the blood could flow
through my veins freely.

After three days
I finally had
the opportunity
to return to Manarma.

I went via Makambisa.
That was where

my brothers had been killed.
That's where you pass
on the way to Manarma.
I did not go alone—
I was not well.
I went together
with my father
and some others.

When we reached Makambisa
that's where we buried my brothers.
We buried others, too.

My stepmother—
whom they had said that they were going to rape
the day before,
the one they took behind the house
and never brought back—
we found her lying dead.
She had a bullet wound.

We buried all these bodies
in Makambisa.
And then we went to Manarma
to bury the rest of the people.
That's why we went there.

When we reached Manarma
the bodies were littered all over.
Bodies of our own people—
people we knew.
We packed them together
so as to bury them.

In Manarma
as we were digging
I told the others
that people had been placed
inside that house.
I said, let us look there.

Let us look there.

We found the people were
completely burned.
We counted the corpses—
they were seventy-three
in number.

We went to bury them.

THE BEGGAR
(TF1-097, RUF Prosecution, November 28, 2005)

As I'm sitting here,
my heart is like when you throw acid
on a piece of cloth,
the way it is shattered,
that's how my heart is—
shattered—
because of what they did to me.

Like when you throw acid
on a piece of cloth.

I was a fisherman
before the war.

I have a wife
and two children.
This is my thirty-seventh year.

Every day, I sit by my brother
in the open-air stall
where he sells small goods—
composition books, pencils,
packets of biscuits, erasers.

I sit there and beg.
My brother gives me some food.
Then I go home.
I am unable
to do anything for myself.

On December twenty-third,
nineteen ninety-eight, around three A.M.,
I was lying down,
asleep.
I woke up in fear,
I woke up and saw fire
on the roof of our home.
I got up and went outside.
I didn't see anyone there.

I went back to my room.
I took my things—
my bag, my tape-player.
All the money I had earned
was in my bag.

The RUF attacked me
at my door.
They took my money,
took the tape-player.
After that, they said I should take the bag,
I should carry the bag on my head.
So I carried the bag on my head
up to the hospital junction.
Captain Blood
said that if I turned to look back,
they would shoot me.

This happened in town.
We ran into the bush.
We stayed in the bush
till daybreak,
six A.M.

Then we decided
to go back to town.
We waited till the place was clear
and when the place was clear, we came.
We came along the peninsula
into the town.

I looked for my brother
but did not find him at home.
I saw the corpses
of seven of my neighbors.
Then we headed toward Freetown
with our people—
it took us five days.

I did not understand Freetown
so I went and stayed in Kissy.
Then, in Kissy,
two weeks later,
January, nineteen ninety-nine,
I was lying down,
and I awakened from sleep
with the intention of going outside
to urinate
and when I went outside
I saw fire.
I was frightened
so I woke up my brother.

I saw people running toward me,
holding bundles on their heads.
It was another RUF attack.
We fled.
We ran through Academy—

it's a school compound,
by Berry Street.
We ran away from Kissy
and came to Berry Street.
We stayed there in that compound
for one week.

We saw the rebels
standing opposite the gates.
They were outside the school compound,
in the street.

After seven days
we ran away.
I told my brother
that I was going to return
to Kissy
because I had nothing to eat
and I wanted to search
for my sister.

That's when I was captured,
at the place where you enter Kissy—
by Ferry Junction, Blackhall Road.
The rebels ordered me to give them money
and I told them I did not have money.
They said that if I don't have money
they will flog me.
They flogged me a dozen times.

The next morning,
when I left that place
to continue on to Kissy
I saw more rebels—

some had machetes,
some had axes,
some had sticks.

I got to Kissy
and I slept.
It was nighttime.
I stayed in my house
for two days.

On the third day,
it was a Wednesday,
January twenty-first,
around two in the afternoon,
I had just come from praying
in the mosque—
two o'clock prayers.

We were inside.
I pushed open the window-curtains.
That's when I saw
a man in combat gear—
he wore a uniform
like that of soldiers from
the SLA.
So I told the others,
if we are going
to be safe from this
in this place
it is only
through the help of God.

We were in the parlor.
The rebels came,

the door was locked,
they said that if we
didn't open the door
they would set the house on fire.
There was no way to escape
so I opened the door.

The man who had attacked me before,
he was called Captain Blood,
the same man attacked me now,
at Kissy.
He asked me to give him
four hundred thousand leones.
I told him I have no money.
He said if I don't give him money
he will cut off my hand.

He stood by the door,
he took the machete,
and struck me with the machete,
on my back, hard.
I fell to the ground.

After that,
he chopped off my hand.
It was Captain Blood
who cut off my hand.

See, everybody,
Everybody that is sitting here
sees that my left hand
has been chopped off.

. . .

After Captain Blood
chopped off my hand
he said that I should
go to President Kabbah,
"Pa Kabbah
will give you hands."

Then another rebel came
and asked, "Where is the money?"
I told him that I had no money.
I told him it would be better
if he would finish me at once.
He said, "We have already finished with you,
so go away."
And he showed me a road.

He showed me a road.

When I was going,
it was midnight
and it was dark.
I was leaning on the wall
of a zinc house—
that's where I leaned.

My hand was still bleeding.
I wanted to drink water.
There was no drinking water,
but there was some toilet water—
that is what I took and drank.
That is how I was able
to revive myself.

I was standing there
for nearly two hours.
I saw someone point a flashlight.
They had flashlights in their hands
because the place was dark.

Only God covered me
where I was leaning.
I was covered by God.
I saw them,
but they did not see me:
God placed a boundary
between me and them.

From where I stood,
leaning, against the wall
of the zinc house,
less than one minute later
I heard people screaming,
"Oh, you are killing me,
you are killing me."
I heard the voices
but I did not see the people
because by then my eyes were dim.

So I climbed a hill
and lay down on
the tangled roots
of a mango tree
and I put my head on a stone.

I saw another house made of zinc,
but God instructed me
not to enter that house

so I went back to
the mango tree
and I rested my head
on that stone.

When I rested my head
I heard the screams
of others whose hands
were being chopped off
and of their sister,
who was being raped.

Out of the shadows
I was shouting
and the townsfolk—
those whose hands had been
chopped off
said, "Who's that?"
I said, "It's me."
They said, "Here is a road—
let's take this road."

Here is a road.

Then we were in the bush.
We spent the whole night there,
till dawn.
In the morning,
we came to Bai Bureh Street.

As I'm sitting here,
my heart is bleeding
like when you take a knife
and stab somebody's heart.

As I'm sitting here now,
my heart is bleeding.

As I'm sitting here,
my heart is like when you throw acid
on a piece of cloth,
the way it is shattered,
that's how my heart is—
shattered—
because of what they did to me.

Like when you throw acid
on a piece of cloth.

Now, things I was doing for myself
I can't do anymore.
I have to pay people to do them for me.
The hard work I was doing for myself,
fishing,
I can no longer do—
now I have turned into a beggar.
I was a fisherman.
Now I have turned into a beggar.
I used to be a fisherman.

Look at me:
I am a young man.
I am a young man.
Who would have known
that I would be like this,
at thirty-seven years?
It's not like I'm fifty or sixty.

I have two children.
Who is taking care of them?
No-one.
Right now, if I ask one of you
for help,
for the school fees for my children,
not one of you will help me.

So if you ask me about
whatever statement I have given
in the past,
if I forget something
or make an error in my testimony,
if you read out my past statement to me,
and refresh my memory,
then you can correct me
and I will answer you

because at the moment, as I'm sitting here,
my heart is bleeding.
My heart is like when you throw acid
on a piece of cloth.

Who would have known
that I would be like this,
at thirty-seven years?

I used to be a fisherman.

THE VICTIM OF WAR

Further Resources

Poetry Collections

Cheney-Coker, Syl. *Stone Child and Other Poems*. HEBN Publishers, 2008. By the winner of the Commonwealth Writers' Prize, Africa region, 1991, and the Fonlon-Nichols Award from the African Literature Association. Cheney-Coker, a native of Sierra Leone, has brought forth five poetry collections, but this is the only one that includes several poems about the civil war.

Wesley, Patricia Jabbeh. *Praise Song for My Children: New and Selected Poems*. Autumn House Press, 2020. The poet is a native of Liberia who fled her homeland during the First Liberian Civil War and now lives in the United States, where she is professor of English and creative writing at Pennsylvania State University. This collection includes many poems about both civil wars in Liberia and thus sheds light on events that were closely entwined with Sierra Leone's war. The Liberian civil wars are also explored in her five previous collections. The poet won a 2002 Crab Orchard Award, and her poems have been nominated four times for the Pushcart Prize.

See also the "Poetry Books" section on the website of the Sierra Leonean Writers Series, https://www.sl-writers-series.org.

Essays and Commentary about Poetry
on the Sierra Leone Civil War

Gberie, Lansana. "A Note on Our Poets: The Burden of Rage and Despair." Article in the newspaper *The Patriotic Vanguard*, October 25, 2009. http://www.thepatrioticvanguard.com/a-note-on-our-poets-the-burden-of-rage-and-despair-4710.

Hallowell, Gbanabom. "On Literary Arts." In *Reinventing Sierra Leone: Literary and Post-Conflict Essays*, pp. 9–88. Africanist Press, 2020.

Lederach, John Paul, and Angela Jill Lederach. "The Poetry of Social Healing." In J. P. Lederach and A. J. Lederach, *When Blood and Bones Cry Out: Journeys through the Soundscape of Healing and Reconciliation*, pp. 170–193. Oxford University Press, 2010.

Porter, Abioseh. "Non-conventional Literary Media: New Poetic Voices on the Internet." In Eustace Palmer and Abioseh Michael Porter, eds., *Knowledge Is More Than Mere Words: A Critical Introduction to Sierra Leonean Literature*, pp. 315–338. Africa World Press, 2008.

Sesay, Mohamed Gibril. "Sierra Leone Literature: History, Hindrances, Hopes." Africanist Press, December 7, 2019. https://africanistpress.com/2019/12/07/sierra-leone-literature-history-hindrances-hopes/.

Skelt, Joanna Kay. "The Social Function of Writing in Post-War Sierra Leone: Poetry as a Discourse for Peace." Thesis submitted to the University of Birmingham for the degree of Doctor of Philosophy, Centre for West African Studies, School of History and Cultures, Birmingham, UK, August 2013. https://core.ac.uk/download/pdf/20123967.pdf.

Walon-Jalloh, Abdulai. *A Review of Salone Poetry*. Sierra Leonean Writers Series, 2019.

Novels

Cheney-Coker, Syl. *Sacred River.* Ohio University Press, 2015. Set in a fictional country reminiscent of Sierra Leone.

Forna, Aminatta. *Ancestor Stones.* Grove Press, 2007. Winner of the Hurston-Wright Legacy Award for Debut Fiction, the Liberaturpreis in Germany, and the Aidoo-Snyder Book Prize; a *New York Times* Editor's Choice book; nominated for the International Dublin IMPAC Award; selected by the *Washington Post* as one of the "Best Novels of 2006" and by *The Listener* magazine as one of the "Best 10 Books of 2006."

———. *The Memory of Love.* Grove Press, 2011. Winner of the Commonwealth Writers' Prize Best Book Award 2011; shortlisted for the Orange Prize for Fiction 2011, the IMPAC Award 2012, and the Warwick Prize 2011; voted one of the "Best Books of the Year" by the *Sunday Telegraph*, *Financial Times*, and *Times* newspapers; a *New York Times* Editor's Choice book; nominated for the European Prize for Fiction 2013.

Hollist, Pede. *So the Path Does Not Die.* African Books Collective, 2012.

Jarrett-Macauley, Delia. *Moses, Citizen and Me.* Granta UK, 2006. Winner of the Orwell Prize 2006.

Short Stories

Conton, Paul. "A Day at the High Court." Published on Kindle, 2019. By the winner of the 1993 Commonwealth Writers Prize for Best First Book.

Hollist, Pede. "Foreign Aid." *Journal of Progressive Human Services* 23 (2013): 258–281. DOI: 10.1080/10428232.2012.725380. https://doi.org/10.1080/10428232.2012.725380. Short-listed for the 2013 Caine Prize for African Writing.

Sesay, Mohamed Gibril. "Half-Man and the Curse of the Ancient Buttocks." In *Work in Progress and Other Stories: The Caine Prize*

for African Writing, 2009, pp. 141–148. New Internationalist
Publications, 2009. Short-listed for the 2009 Caine Prize.

Terry, Olufemi. "Stickfighting Days." In *A Life in Full and Other
Stories: The Caine Prize for African Writing, 2010*, pp. 59–75. New
Internationalist Publications, 2010. The story is set in an
unnamed West African country, but the themes, characters, and
images are evocative of post–civil war Freetown. Winner of the
2010 Caine Prize.

Children's and Young Adult Fiction

Conteh, Osman. *Unanswered Cries*. Macmillan UK, 2001. Focuses
on female genital cutting, but also sheds light on broader
cultural and gender-related norms. Winner of Macmillan
Children's Literature Award, Senior Section.

Forna, Namina. *The Gilded Ones*. Delacorte Press, 2021. The author
was born and raised in Sierra Leone until age ten. The story is set
in a fantasized West African milieu that is suggestive of Sierra
Leone; the themes of gender-based violence and eventual
liberation are reminiscent of the experiences of many young
women during the civil war.

See also the website of the Sierra Leonean Writers Series for
additional books for children, adolescents, and young adults.

Memoirs and Literary Nonfiction

Beah, Ishmael. *A Long Way Gone: Memoirs of a Boy Soldier*. Farrar,
Straus & Giroux, 2007.

Forna, Aminatta. *The Devil That Danced on the Water: A Daughter's
Quest*. Grove Press, 2003. Runner-up for the Samuel Johnson
Prize 2003; chosen for the Barnes & Noble Discover New
Writers Series; serialized on BBC Radio and in the *Sunday*

Times newspaper. The author was the 2014 winner of the Windham Campbell Prize.

———. *The Window Seat: Notes From a Life in Motion*. Grove Press, 2021.

Kamara, Mariatu, and Susan McClelland. *The Bite of the Mango*. Annick Press, 2008.

Oral Storytelling

Wurie, Fatou. "When the Heart Is Full." The Moth, Stories, 2017. https://themoth.org/stories/when-the-heart-is-full.

Drama

Christensen, Matthew J., ed. *Staging the Amistad: Three Sierra Leonean Plays*. Ohio University Press, 2019. Dramas by Sierra Leonean playwrights Charlie Haffner, Yulisa Amadu "Pat" Maddy, and Raymond de'Souza George.

Osagie, Iyunolu, ed. *Theater in Sierra Leone: Five Popular Plays*. Africa World Press, 2009.

See also *Ruined* by Lynn Nottage, winner of the 2009 Pulitzer Prize for Drama. This play is set in the Democratic Republic of Congo, not in Sierra Leone, but it depicts women who suffered vesicovaginal fistulas as a result of wartime rape, a type of traumatic war injury that is common among sexual violence survivors in Sierra Leone. (VVF is a chronic condition portrayed in this volume by the speaker in the poem "The Rape Survivor.")

Literary Criticism

Cole, Ernest. *Space and Trauma in the Writings of Aminatta Forna*. Africa World Press, 2016.

Palmer, Eustace. Introduction to *Knowledge Is More Than Mere Words: A Critical Introduction to Sierra Leonean Literature*, pp. 1–33. Edited by Eustace Palmer and Abioseh Michael Porter. Africa World Press, 2008.

Palmer, Eustace, and Ernest Cole. *Emerging Perspectives on Syl Cheney-Coker*. Africa World Press, 2014.

Online Creative Writing by Sierra Leoneans

Hollist, Pede. *Pede Hollist's Literature Blog: Narrating Everyday Sierra Leone*. https://pede-hollist.com. Hollist, originally from Sierra Leone, is a writer and a professor of English at the University of Tampa. Accepts submissions of poetry, nonfiction, fiction, and proverbs to be made available online.

Leonenet (an online forum for Sierra Leoneans and persons interested in Sierra Leone), "Literary Arts and Music" section. To subscribe, email the administrators at leoneadm@umbc.edu.

www.sierra-leone.org/poetry.html. This website about Sierra Leonean history and culture features many poems written by Sierra Leoneans. The site administrator is the former spokesperson for the Special Court, Peter Anderson. To submit original poems, e-mail Andersen@sierra-leone.org.

Young Writers Sierra Leone Facebook Group. To join, send an e-mail to youngwriterssl@yahoo.co.uk.

General and Miscellaneous

Book Aid International. "Inspiring Readers Sierra Leone," in partnership with the Sierra Leone Library Board, Phase 1 report, July 24, 2019. https://bookaid.org/wp-content/uploads/2019/07/IR-Sierra-Leone-phase-1-final-eval-FOR-WEB.pdf. See also Book Aid International's Country Report for Sierra Leone at https://bookaid.org/countries/sierra-leone/.

Palmer, Eustace, and Porter, Abioseh Michael, eds. "Select Bibliography: Primary Works, Secondary Sources." In *Knowledge Is More Than Mere Words: A Critical Introduction to Sierra Leonean Literature*, pp. 339–351. Africa World Press, 2008.

PEN International, Sierra Leone Centre. https://pen-international .org/centres/sierra-leone-centre.

Sierra Leonean Writers Series, an academic and general publisher established in post–civil war Freetown, focusing on works by Sierra Leoneans and others who write about Sierra Leone. Has published over 100 books, in all literary genres. Website contains information about SLWS's books and authors. https://www.sl -writers-series.org/index.php/en/.

Smith, Arthur. "Looking Back on the Path of the Literary Arts in Sierra Leone," October 7, 2007. https://ezinearticles.com /?Looking-Back-On-The-Path-Of-The-Literary-Arts-In-Sierra -Leone&id=770650.

Spencer, Sylvanus. *Promoting Freedom of Expression in Post-War Sierra Leone*. Sierra Leonean Writers Series, 2019.

The official transcripts of the trials conducted by the Special Court for Sierra Leone are available to the public via the archives of the Residual Special Court (www.rscsl.org). Additional SCSL materials comprising documents and videos can be found at www.scsldocs.org.

The full report of Sierra Leone's Truth and Reconciliation Commission (TRC) (a separate entity from the Special Court) is available online at sierraleonetrc.org. For a summary, see http://sierraleonetrc .org/index.php/view-the-final-report.

Acknowledgments

"The Child Soldier," "The Grieving Father," and "The Grave-digger" were published in three separate issues of *J Journal: New Writing on Justice* in 2011 and 2012 under slightly different titles. In 2015, an earlier version of "The Amputee's Mother" was published in the *Doctor T. J. Eckleburg Review* under a slightly different title after winning third prize in that journal's 2014 contest for the Gertrude Stein Award. "The Blinded Farmer," "The Widower," "The Beggar," and "The Victim of War" were combined into a single piece, titled "Three Witnesses from the Special Court for Sierra Leone and One Silence," which won first prize for the 2017 Gabriele Rico Award in Creative Nonfiction, sponsored by *Reed Magazine*. That piece was published in *Reed Magazine*'s 150th anniversary issue in May 2017.

Sincere appreciation to Alrick Brown for sharing his literary insights during the early phases of this project. Eternal gratitude to Lila Coleburn for her abiding commitment to my growth as a writer and person. Special thanks to Brenda Hillman for inviting me to present portions of this work on a panel she chaired at the annual conference of the Association of Writers and Writing Programs in 2010. Heartfelt praise to Emily Shearer for providing wise guidance on the introduction and for convincing me that these voices need to be heard.

Laurie Sheck provided astute feedback on initial drafts of these poems, and helped me to recognize new possibilities for poetic craft and to honor and hone my vision for this project. Papay Solomon applied his rare talent to the creation of the painting that appears on the cover. Yana Serry helped me discern the nuances of many Krio words in the transcripts and offered countless moments of joy to counterbalance the sorrow I absorbed while working on these poems.

I was given a blessing, however brief, in having reached out to Carmen R. Gillespie in March 2019 to ask if she would consider publishing this work. Dr. Gillespie—poet, literary scholar, professor of English, and founder and director of the Griot Institute for Africana Studies at Bucknell University—was the editor of the Griot Project Book Series, and without her early encouragement and receptivity, this book would not exist. In spring 2019 she read some sample poems, and then the work as a whole, and in July she committed to sending the manuscript out for peer review. I knew I would learn much from her. Alas, those plans were cut short in August 2019 by her untimely passing. However, I view this book as part of her legacy, and would be honored if others would as well.

I am immensely grateful to the staff at Bucknell University Press and the Griot Project Book Series for believing in the importance of this book and for their professionalism and hard work, which have remained constant even in the midst of a global pandemic. In particular, I thank Pamelia Dailey, the press's managing editor, for her assiduous support with permissions, manuscript preparation, cover design, and the countless other steps that were important in shepherding this project to fruition. Most especially, I could not have imagined a more remarkable editor than Suzanne E. Guiod, director and editor in chief at the press, who generously stepped in to carry the project forward after Carmen died. Suzanne has shown prodigious amounts of patience, conscientiousness, insight, talent, and erudition while editing this book. In addition, Suzanne thoughtfully recruited two anonymous reviewers who read the manuscript with exceptional attentiveness and skill and made many helpful suggestions. For all this and more, I am indebted to her beyond measure.

I am obliged to Daryl Brower, my production editor at Rutgers University Press, and her gifted colleagues, for their responsiveness and care during the course of producing this book. Barbara Goodhouse—copyeditor supreme—displayed dedication and adroitness in her work on the manuscript. Angela Piliouras, my production editor at Westchester Publishing Services, brought kindness, energy, and a sincere commitment to excellence while preparing the manuscript for publication.

Finally, my deepest acknowledgment goes to the witnesses from the Special Court for Sierra Leone. In sharing the truth of their experiences, they demonstrated extraordinary courage, resilience, and generosity of spirit. I continue to draw inspiration from their example.

About the Cover Artist

PAPAY SOLOMON is a Liberian war refugee born in Guinea who now lives and paints in Phoenix, Arizona. His mother, while pregnant with him, fled the First Liberian Civil War to seek refuge in Guinea. When he was a child, armed paramilitary factions embroiled in the Second Liberian Civil War and the Sierra Leone Civil War attacked the town in which he and his mother and sister had settled. As a result, they were relocated to a refugee camp in a remote forest region that lacked basic services and supplies.

When he was ten years old, Mr. Solomon's artistic talent came to the attention of Shanee Stepakoff during her year-long position as a human rights defender in the camp, as she observed him sketching on random scraps of paper with the limited writing instruments available. After learning about their war-related losses, Dr. Stepakoff referred the Solomon family for resettlement in the United States. In 2008, Mr. Solomon, along with his mother, his sister, and his sister's infant son, arrived in Phoenix, where he entered high school. In May 2018 he obtained his bachelor of fine arts degree from Arizona State University, where he also received the Outstanding Undergraduate Award.

Mr. Solomon is now a rising star of the regional and national art scene. He specializes in large-scale hyperrealistic portraits of young Black men and women, in particular immigrants and refugees from the African continent. His use of hyperrealism reflects the double consciousness that many people of African origin who reside in the United States report as part of their daily experience. In most of his work, he also uses elements of non finito to visually represent the sense of incompleteness and in-betweenness that is common among Africans in the diaspora.

Mr. Solomon won the 2018 Friends of Contemporary Art Artists' Grant and Award from the Phoenix Art Museum; his paintings were then displayed at the museum for seven months. His work has been featured in *Phoenix Home and Garden*, *International Artists*, *American Art Collector*, and *Critical Multilingualism Studies*. In *New American Paintings*, he was Editor's Choice and was featured on the cover. He had his first solo exhibition, "African for the First Time," at the Joseph Gross Gallery in Tucson, Arizona, from January to March 2020. His work was shown at the Tucson Museum of Art as part of the 2018 Arizona Biennial Exhibition. One of his paintings was selected from nearly 2,000 entries to be shown at the National Portrait Gallery in London beginning in May 2020. In fall 2020, he had his second solo exhibition at Steven Zevitas Gallery in Boston, and his work was featured in *The Boston Globe*.

Mr. Solomon continues to flourish as a painter focusing on using the visual arts to express the dignity, beauty, and resilience of persons of African descent. Consistent with his long-term efforts to integrate visual and verbal forms of storytelling, he kindly offered to create the painting that appears on the cover of this book.

About the Foreword Author

ERNEST D. COLE is John Dirk Werkman Professor of English at Hope College in Holland, Michigan. His research focuses primarily on postapartheid South Africa, but he is also interested in body and trauma studies, especially the ways in which bodily injury shapes identity. He is the author of several books, including *Space and Trauma in the Writings of Aminatta Forna* and *Theorizing the Disfigured Body: Mutilation, Amputation, and Disability Culture in Post Conflict Sierra Leone*.

About the Author

SHANEE STEPAKOFF is a clinical psychologist, human rights advocate, and scholar with extensive experience in Guinea, Liberia, Sierra Leone, South Africa, and other postwar settings. She holds an MFA in creative writing from the New School and is currently completing a second PhD, in English, at the University of Rhode Island. Her writing has been published in the *Dr. T. J. Eckleburg Review*, *Reed Magazine*, and three issues of *J Journal: New Writing on Justice*, as well as in eight edited books. She won first prize in *Reed Magazine*'s 2017 Gabrielle Rico Creative Nonfiction Award. She was the third-place winner of *Eckleburg*'s 2014 Gertrude Stein Award. Dr. Stepakoff is also the author of more than fifteen academic essays and articles, which have been published in the *International Journal of Transitional Justice*, *The Drama Review*, *The Arts in Psychotherapy*, *Journal of Human Rights Practice*, *American Psychologist*, *Swift Studies*, and other journals.